I'll bet every one of us at one time or another has amazed and amused a whole room full of people with an almost unbelievable story full of craziness, daring, humour or tragedy. When someone asks you in disbelief, you say, 'Of course it's true! The people involved are friends of a friend's friend. And my mate swears that it really happened.' If only you were able to say, 'Well, actually, I was there...' or 'It was me.'

Well, this guy really was there. It actually was him.

Eric Gooden, Bush Records

Ascension is a check on reality, life in all its detail. To read an honest account of somebody else's ups and downs can be refreshing, but can make you deal with lots of issues along the way. *Ascension* will challenge you, and make you thankful you survived intact and relatively sane.

Tim Lennox, Cream/Golden

Being a former partaker in the rave scene, not taking drugs but having many friends who did, I felt that this story was the closest one could get to actually living (or in my case re-living) the experience. The book seems to draw you in unapologetically and subject you to a time of great dance tunes, sweaty dance raves and 'ACEEEEEEEEED'. Great read.

Big Ben, Phats and Small

ASCENSION

CLUBS, DRUGS AND
THE ETERNAL HIGH

Cameron Dante
with Craig Borlase

GRAND RAPIDS, MICHIGAN 49530

ZONDERVAN™

Ascension
Copyright © 2001 by Cameron Dante and Craig Borlase

Cameron Dante and Craig Borlase assert the moral right to be identified as the authors of this work.

First published in Great Britain in 2001 by HarperCollins*Publishers*

Requests for information should be addressed to:
Zondervan, *Grand Rapids, Michigan 49530*

A catalog record for this book is available from the British Library.

ISBN 0-00-710517-7

Printed and bound in Great Britain by Omnia Books Limited, Glasgow.

01 02 03 04 05 06 /❖/ 5 4 3 2

Dedicated to the party generation
seeking out the ultimate high.
Where is it?
Are you looking in the right place?

CONTENTS

THANKS

I would like to thank:

my family, who are the most understanding and precious people
    I know on this earth
the Hawthorne family for being mates beyond the call of duty
Zark and Miriam Porter for beginning the journey with me
Steve and Helen Cockram for continuing the journey with me
the Ascension team
Mum, Dad, Paul and Michael, who are my grounding, and
last but not least Craig Borlase without whom this book wouldn't
    have happened.

FOREWORD

You know all those things you always wanted to do but were afraid to? The things that could have brought trouble your way? The things that you knew were wrong, but you just wanted to try anyway? We all knew someone who did them and often got away with them, didn't we?

Well now, from the safety of your armchair, you can read *Ascension* and experience the adventure of growing up and taking risks. That's what it's all about. It's about having a laugh. But more often than not the consequences have to be dealt with ... and they're trouble enough.

Our hero takes drugs and does some nasty things – he's not a hero in the true sense of the word. As I said, it's an adventure, but not in the traditional sense. It's real life, and we all know what an adventure or a danger that can be. Live it without fear, but live it with wisdom and enjoy the discovery of youth.

This is the best history lesson you'll ever have!

Graeme Park, DJ, Galaxy

INTRODUCTION

Rebellion was the new language of the late 80s in the inner city. As we watched people screaming and shouting at each other on the TV in *Wall Street*, it seemed as if everyone was getting rich except us. Then came the biggest underground movement to hit this country since the 60s. The music was the genesis, the illegal parties were the gospel, and the drugs were the revelation. What more could any one need from life?

With police raids becoming the norm we were really pissing the Government off. They couldn't contain us. They couldn't maintain us, and they certainly couldn't refrain from letting us get away with it. It was my heaven.

This book had to be toned down a little bit to stop it sounding like a pharmaceutical dictionary. Yet life did seem like one long binge. Some of the people I met along the way are still buzzing, but you'll hear them say the buzz isn't the same. Some of the characters in the book have lost the battle, but some like Ian are winning. We were the product of a new generation searching for the ultimate buzz. Was something missing? Maybe...

PLAYBACK

This is me. Decks in front, crouched down between two spinning globes, life moving at the perfect bpm. The time it takes for the next record to play through could well be the time it takes to tell my story: the journey from early days in the pram to present-day Cam has been long, but not so long that I couldn't burn, roll and pack it down into a tastily packaged four-minute affair. But that'd be no fun. Cam's always had an ear for a good tale, and I might as well put it to good use here. Pay attention at the back! I'll be asking questions afterwards ...

'And the trams are running slow today due to industrial action.' Sorry about that. Handing out traffic information is one of the perks of the job. I'm bolted into a six by eight sound-proofed booth at Kiss 102. It's 7.15 a.m. and ...

'It's 7.15. It's Saturday morning and you're listening to Cameron Dante on Kiss 102 FM. This is Robert Owens.'

Another perk. My mind wanders while I'm in here. There's something about the set-up that acts as fertilizer for the imagi-nation. I find myself going off on all sorts of mental day-trips: just last week I spent the entire three-hour slot trying to dream

1

up decent names for any kids I might have in the future. Kid Infringement Happy Dante. Maybe not.

This is week three of my incarnation as Cameron Dante, Weekend Breakfast Show DJ, and so far the slot hasn't been too bad. It all started when, just a few weeks ago, I got asked to take over the Sunday morning show, the Holy Graveyard as the producer called it. Yeah, it was nice to be asked, but then again I suppose there wasn't that much competition for the gig. I didn't kill anyone during those first few shows and they offered me this Saturday gig as well. Perhaps not the best slot a DJ could hope for, but still, the way I see it is that this is a chance to ramble on about pretty much what I want in between playing my favourite tunes. And if nothing else it's a decent way of keeping in touch with your mates.

'Big shout out to the Old Skool Vinny.'

I got the slot for a couple of reasons. First I can mix. It wasn't always the case, and my first experiences of being in a DJ booth were far more Club 18-30 than I'd like to admit. I was there, leading the chant for the conga, judging the assets for the wet T-shirt competition. Not nice. But it got better with time, and by 1989 I was a fully signed up member of the baggy scene. No more singalongs and sticky dance floors for Cam; the club scene had got me by the short and curlies and there was no way I was going back. E, Hacienda, service stations ... you know the script.

I got the first gig with Kiss 102 because I've tasted the eternal high. Never used to be bothered about it before, despite the roots. Nah, all that sort of stuff was something that I'd left at the bottom of the wardrobe along with the school books and waffle jumpers. The way I played it for most of my life was on a solely Me First tip. What happened? Well, let's just say things changed a month ago. Confused? Relax; it'll all come clear in the end.

A light on the desk tells me there's a phone call coming in. I'm still a bit new to the technology so I hope whoever it is doesn't want to be put through on air. Check the record; Bobby Owens is still offering eternal friendship and it looks like he'll be at it for a good 30 seconds yet. Just time for a quick chat.

'Cameron speaking.'

'Awlrightmate?' An impression of a Mancunian drawl that camp could only come from one person.

'Ian, you old queen.' I guess right.

'Get that handbag anthem off the radio and put on some real tunes.'

End of conversation. I like Ian. He keeps things simple. He'll have just got home having enjoyed a night and three quarters soaking up the highs and lows with the rest of the Canal Street mafia. It's becoming a little ritual we have; he gets home early Saturday morning, puts on the radio and calls me with some specific abuse. I strike back.

'And there's another letter in this week from Ian in Strangeways, asking to hear Shanice and "I Love Your Smile". This one's for you, big boy.'

Like I said, last week got taken up with thinking about names for kids. I don't know why – there don't seem to be any on the way – but that's just the kind of mood I've been in lately. I've been on one of those mind excursions, taking in some of the sights of my life. The Leaning Tower of Sanity. The Grand Canyon of Drug Abuse. The Mountain Peaks and Valleys of Cameron Dante Aged 0 to 31.

The show played out with a couple more hoax calls of encouragement from Ian, too many adverts and me getting semi-excited to discover that someone had left a copy of Little Louis' 'French Kiss' in the corner of the studio. I made my way back from the studios to my flat, stopping for paper, fags and milk, just like I had last week. Happy that I'd just set myself up with a new ritual, I walked the last half-mile home as slow as I could without looking as though I was on medication.

ASCENSION

It's a thoughtful time that I'm going through right now. Everything's been going through so much change over the last few months that at times I just have to do this slow walking thing to try and take it all in. I've already put an end to my drug taking and have shifted my ambitions around pretty much 180 degrees. I'm scared of losing myself in it all, of going through so much change that I'll not have a clue who it'll be that comes out on the other side.

And so my whole life story has been on slow playback on the back wall of my mind. Frame by frame – missing out the sections that have been edited out by Uncle Amnesia and the crew – but the show's almost all there. Take it away boys.

P.S. Call just in on the mobile. After the ritual struggle of trying to get the oversized device out of my undersized jacket pocket I managed to take the call. It was some producer from Radio One, said he wondered whether I'd be into taking on the odd guest slot, starting with a Christmas Eve Massive. Was I keen? Just a bit.

CRIME

It all started in Cheetham Hill, one of the rougher sides of Salford, which is the roughest side of Manchester. The council had rammed the place with two types of people: blacks and Irish. My parents fell into the second group and I grew up knowing that strange type of safety that comes with living around violence. Doors were always left open and the streets were safe. No one ever brought their work home.

But I'm going too fast here. My dad – Michael Newton – was from the west coast of Ireland, and he met Veronica, my Dubliner mum, back on the Emerald Isle. When her family moved over to Manchester towards the end of the 60s, the heart strings were wound so tight that my dad had to do the right thing and move over as well. They had no money, but with a risky win at the bookies threatening to burst his wallet, my dad proposed and they got married. Apparently he was so bladdered on the wedding night that he spent the night sleeping in the bath.

This was the way it was with my family, and everyone always took things well. I can't imagine what it must have been like to grow up in a family where fights took place all the time. Mine was a loving home, and even though the lack of money brought a fair few pressures along with it, happiness always seemed to come out on top. In case you're wondering, I changed my name from Newton to Dante when I started getting into the music industry. After all, Newton just doesn't quite work, does it?

My dad's a real thinker but he's also the type who wouldn't say boo to a goose. He worked for British Rail for 25 years and was nearly always doing shift work. He left without much to show for it, just a few pennies really. He was a full-on blagger and he knew how to skive with the best of them. Many's the time when he'd clock on at 10 p.m. and be back at home by midnight. He just knew how to make it work, how not to let the system get him down.

But if my dad's the laid-back one, my mum, well, she's hard as nails and would knock anyone out if she felt that she needed to stand up for something. I suppose I take more after her, probably not quite as hard, but I grew up knowing that some things were worth fighting for, especially family. She was loving and understanding too, and I can remember being sent into town to collect the wages from my dad one week. I must have only been about 10, and I had to go up on the bus. Coming back I got confused, forgot where I had to get off and managed to lose that week's wages. I crept back home, expecting my mum to be mad as hell, but she was fine. She knew it was just a mistake and she said no more about it. Other kids would have got a beating, but I just got a hug.

So there was me and my brother, Michael. He was younger and more like my dad. He was – and still is – quieter than me, but the bond has always been strong. I'd stick up for him, but I'd always tell him to try and fight his own battles first. If he still needed me I'd be there, but – and this must have come from Mum – standing up for yourself was always worth doing.

Even though me and Michael were the only members of the family's younger generation for years, things changed further on

6

down the line. I must have been about 15 at the time and my mum had a bad attack of psoriasis, a nasty illness she had had for some years that needed plenty of hospital treatment. She was about four or five weeks into the radiotherapy when the doctors hit her with some unexpected news: she was pregnant. Considering the treatment and all that, the hospital were keen for her to terminate the pregnancy, but she dug her heels in.

'I didn't get put on this earth to flush a child of mine down the loo.'

I remember her saying that almost every day for a couple of weeks. It was her mantra, all her beliefs wrapped up into one neat little sentence. Even though I was plenty old enough to understand exactly what it was she was talking about, my mind helped out with the interpretation by conjuring up images of sandalled feet sticking up out of the toilet bowl. I never saw a head, just two scruffy-looking feet with maybe some scabby knees attached if my mind was particularly active.

Mum's determination to keep the baby did wonders for me. It wasn't just this child inside her that she was fighting for; she was saying a massive YES to all her kids. Much of it was about her Catholic faith, but deep down she knew that if there was a child inside of her it deserved the right to life. Not that it was all stress-free, and I can remember seeing her in tears for the first time. It shook me to see her like that, but we all knew she was making the right decision. A few months later I had a new little brother, Paul, and he's turned out to be a top lad.

I suppose that what comes later on in this book, the behaviour and all that, might make you think that I'd had a bad upbringing. But confusing poverty with a lack of love or knowledge is always a dangerous thing. At the end of the day, debt may have been a constant presence and the debt men may have always been knocking at the door, but money, or lack of it, was never the most important thing in life. We may have been poor, but we had something money couldn't buy. Love. How sweet.

That's enough of that. As my first decade came to an end the whole family were moved from the familiarity of Cheetham Hill to Wythenshawe. It was only about nine or ten miles, but the chance of moving into a new house was something my mum couldn't pass up.

The first few hours for a kid in a new area can be crucial; so much to do and so little time in which to do it. My brother bottled it and stayed indoors but I knew I had to get out there and make a name for myself in this foreign jungle. While my parents were unpacking the cases, I untangled my jacket from the pile of my clothes that had been dumped in the middle of my new room and headed outside.

I'd not seen it on the way in, but the house next door was something special. I don't mean that it was much different from the rest, but it seemed to have pulled quite a crowd. There were three cars crushed onto the front garden and the door was half open. I thought I could make out some shouting inside and, being a curious type, I squeezed my way between the bumpers and got closer to the front door so that I'd be able to hear better.

'You're lucky that you're too young to look like a copper,' said a voice behind me.

I froze on the doorstep as a hand landed itself on my shoulder. It turned me around and I could see that it belonged to a lad who looked like he was 15 but wanted to be thought of as 20.

'Well, you're lucky I don't smash your face in with my strongest punch,' went the reply in my head. First impressions count and I was not about to let the side down.

'Sorry mate, I'm new here,' came my blubbing, high-pitched reply. Damn. Why didn't I just smack him one? Why hadn't I made it clear right from the start that this was my patch now and he'd better watch out?

'Just mind your business, awlright?'

I just about managed to hold back the tears enough to squeak out a 'thank you' and legged it back through the graveyard of cars to the safe haven of our new home. Thankfully the others were too busy unpacking to notice my state of nervous tension and I went back to the pile of clothes in my room, playing the situation through in my mind, each time with an alternative, violent and victorious.

By chance we'd happened to move in next door to a family who were a big name on the local crime scene. They'd taken a shine to the place and had bought up a few of the houses in our row, getting other members of their family in as soon as possible. Within days we found out that we were all right though, as one of their less favoured relatives was trying to wedge her way into our gaff. The family weren't exactly keen and told my mum that they'd do what they could to help us stay. So while others were scared, we were fine, and after the initial shock of the move, I got on with the job of growing up feeling nice and secure.

Wythenshawe was as rough as Cheetham Hill. At night the police sirens added their bit of local colour and the news of shootings, stabbings or some other kind of violent revenge never seemed that far away. Of course, most of the stories focused in on our neighbours, but they were always nice to us, so we just got on with stuff.

As a good Catholic lad I went to Cathedral RC secondary school. It seemed that it was the real dossers' school, that everyone who'd been chucked out of all the other schools wound up there, at the bottom of the pile. I was there with Vinny, my best mate since as long as I can remember. We spent all our time at each other's houses, and as we grew up, we settled into a routine of life at secondary school: have a laugh, get in trouble and smoke. Smoking was a big thing, and Vinny and I were good at it. By the time we sauntered through the gates at Cathedral, pack of Embassy in hand, we knew that we would be welcome in the smokers' corner.

Thinking about it now, this last-resort school really was up against it. They must have been so keen to keep it going that they put up with the very worst types of behaviour. Maybe they knew we had nowhere else to go and that kicking us out of there was as good as taking us straight to the canal and dumping us in. But they hung on, still keeping an eye out, still soaking up the cheek and the abuse that got handed out on a daily basis.

Me and Vinny had put the work in during our pre-teen years. We'd been making sure that we were accomplished trouble-makers, and as soon as we arrived we were ready to prove just how much extra-curricular effort we'd been putting in to being a pair of grade A turkeys. Like any good adventure story we had a villain too, although ours came not in the form of some twitching Nazi or cat-stroking, one-eyed psychopath, but as Mr Drennan, headmaster. We hated him and he hated us. He was a tetchy little fella, and just walking into school in my best punk outfit – the mohican, the 18-hole DMs and all that – seemed to be enough to send me back home for another three-day suspension.

But Vinny and I were just sheep. We needed someone to look up to, someone to follow, as without fresh input our tricks soon got stale. Then came Chris. He was bolder, madder and a lot more dominant. I learnt how to look after myself and found out everything that I thought I needed to know about life through Chris. He had that air of authority, the sort that made people listen when he opened his mouth, ready to take it on board. He might have carried on like that too, but a police-car chase put an end to it all. He died some years ago.

The first time Vinny and I met him was when we were 12. We bumped into him during the day at school, got talking and before long he made us an offer.

'Fancy doing a couple of cars one night, lads?'

Of course we both pretended that we knew what he was going on about, but secretly we were both totally confused by what specific type of 'doing' we were going to do to these cars. Were we going to paint them? A quick wash and wax, perhaps? I wondered.

'Oh yeah, Chris,' said Vinny. 'That's if Cam's allowed out.' They both looked at me and laughed. I went red and looked for something to kick.

We arranged to meet near his house at 1 a.m. I'd pretended to go to bed earlier, but had spent hours getting my outfit just right: black balaclava, black trousers and a nicely dirty brown roll-neck jumper. I crept out feeling like I was about to pull off the heist of the century, but as soon as I saw an identically dressed Vinny down the street, I knew I probably didn't look quite as cool as I'd hoped. By the way he was laughing I could tell he felt the same.

Chris was a proper scally, and he'd made sure that he was prepared. When we met him he led us straight away to a row of parked cars, all of which he tested to see whether they'd been left unlocked. None had, so out came a strip of that webbed packing tape you get wrapped around bundles of newspapers. He selected a car, turned his back on us and within a minute he was in. Vinny and I were amazed, and for a brief moment we let our guard down. Instead of appearing as though nicking cars was the most natural thing in the world to us, we both stood with our mouths wide open, balaclavas stretched to the max. Chris looked back, laughed and jumped in the car. After more rustling from inside he quickly came out with the radio, which he put in a plastic bag and hid in a nearby bush.

'Fancy a drive, lads?' he asked. Chris was one of life's salesmen. Everything he ever did was sales, and he had persuading impressionable teenagers down to a fine art. Every sentence I ever heard him utter seemed to start with 'fancy a ...' and he always had some scam or other on the go. Of course, what

11

self-respecting scally could ever turn down any offer like the ones Chris kept up his sleeve? He had us hooked.

'Fancy a drive,' he said, 'or have you bottled it?'

Vinny and I were still standing in shock, but we managed to climb into the back without too much difficulty. We sat in the back and heard even more rustling, although this time it was accompanied by a loud crack, a bit of swearing and the biggest fright of my young life as the engine howled its way into life. I don't know what else I was expecting it to do, but the hot-wiring brought me out of my trance and into an adrenaline-fuelled rush unlike any I'd experienced before.

'Not good,' I thought.

Chris drove the Mk II Escort round the corner to what was supposed to be the local football pitch. In reality it was a strip of waste land that people occasionally used to dump furniture and whatever else they didn't want, and it wasn't the most sensible place for us to be. It was bordered on three sides by flats, and there was only one way in and out of it. If the Old Bill had come along just one car would have been enough to trap us. Chris was flinging the car about the rec, doing handbrake turns and all that, and one by one the lights in the flats came on as angry-sounding silhouettes screamed at us to shut up and clear off. The audience only added to the excitement and we kept it up for as long as we could. At the time it was a top buzz, but the finale was yet to come: Chris did an almighty turn that slammed the side of the car into a wall. We all jumped out, Chris pulled a long rag from out of his jacket and shoved one end of it in the petrol tank. He lit the other end and we ran to the trees. Within minutes the car was in flames and we were roasting off the heat of the Mk II as well as the buzz of a naughty job well done. We walked the half-mile home going over the past 30 minutes in microscopic detail, Vinny and I trying desperately to convince Chris that we'd done that sort of thing before. We split up and each went back to our beds, not thinking that we had done anything wrong, just thinking we'd been a bit naughty.

The next day was different. We wanted to get to school. This was no sudden sense of guilt, mind you, no result of a cold sweat in the middle of the night realizing that our young lives were about to take a turn for the worse that could only be fought off with hard work and a commitment to study and self-improvement. Nah mate, we wanted to show off. We were titchy little first-years at the time and life was tough. It was a jungle out there and you had to fight for your position. We made sure that by first break everyone knew that the smouldering car they had seen on the way in was the result of yours truly. Like true businessmen we knew how to strike when opportunity came knocking. Dicky Branson would have been proud.

We worked hard on making a name for ourselves, and the effort paid off: Vinny and I became known as proper little scallies, and what with the fact that we already smoked and knew about punk music, we were laughing. But in our little gang we were still the sheep, and the shepherd was doing a good job with his flock. Chris became an icon, the man that Vinny and I looked up to. He'd been there, done it and knew how to keep us in adrenaline.

We were at it for a few weeks. Soon Vinny and I took our turns behind the wheel, kangarooing down the road. Chris would always seem to drive harder and faster once his young pupils had had a go themselves, and even though we didn't need any reminding, his spins, crashes and burnouts kept his place warm at the top of the pile.

Soon we knew it was time to move. Burnt-out cars and the like weren't exactly regular occurrences round our way – or at least they weren't until us three musketeers started up. As I said before, there were plenty of people who made their money from 'alternative' sources living round our way, but none of them was

13

ever that keen on homework. The crimes that took place – mild and mindless as they might have seemed to us – were gradually causing a bit of a stir. It just wasn't the done thing, and soon the police were doing regular patrols around the rec at night. For a while we'd take our transport down to the railway, but the lack of audience somehow made it slightly less appealing.

But Chris had opened a treasure chest of opportunity, and the next jewel for us to get our grubby little mitts on bore a name that sparked excitement in any young lad's heart: Dixons. And by now it wasn't just Vinny and me, as our little gang had been through a bit of a growth spurt. We'd taken on Adam Walker and Dean. Can't remember much about old Deano now, but Wacko is still large in my mind. He was brought in to fill that most important of roles: the goon. Every gang needs one and Mr Walker was the man for us. He put up with no end of abuse, and as far as we were concerned he was there to be torn apart. From the way he dressed to the way he walked, from his mum to his name, we showed no mercy. He got a rough deal from us, but still he came back for more. I feel sorry for him now and there's no excuse.

'Wacko,' we'd start up whenever there was a lull in the conversation, 'you know that porno video your brother's got/money your mum gave you/bike your cousin lent you ...'

Wacko would groan and look blankly at us, like some ageing family cat that knew it was about to receive its daily dose of torment at the hands of the snotty kids. And so we'd bend, bribe and abuse Wacko any way which suited us. Normally it meant him acting as waiter to our unquenchable appetites, but occasionally we'd beat him up so that he could have a bit of fun.

So as I was saying, we were just about getting bored with the old smash 'n' burn when the Dixons plan came into view. Being 12 years old meant that we loved anything to do with electricals, and the thought of coming out with an armful of Walkmans was enough to have me do something really stupid, like rob a fully alarmed store in broad daylight. The plan was simple, said Chris: we'd rob the store on Regent Road at 5.05 p.m. as soon as they'd shut (he wanted to get back for his tea or something). Oh, and it was alarmed.

Of course this sounded like a great plan. We'd seen enough films by then to know that all you had to do to get around an alarm was cut the black wire. Or was it the red? Anyway, some wire cutting was involved and after that it was a stroll in the park, just a question of loading the gear into a van and speeding off. But here was our masterstroke. Everyone would be expecting us to use a van – probably a white one too – so we were going to do the unexpected. Instead of making our getaway by motor, we would do it by shopping trolley. After all, what would look more normal than three 12-year-olds pushing trolleys crammed with boxes of electrical goods down the street? And to think, this was even before we'd got into donating huge amounts of brain cells to glue sniffing. With that little intellect at the start it's a wonder I still know how to walk.

So there we were, outside the back of the Regent Road branch with a couple of shopping trolleys. There was a lot of redevelopment going on at the time, and every building behind it had been knocked down. Somehow Vinny wasn't there – perhaps he wasn't quite as thick as Chris and me – and it was far too exciting a job to let Dean and Wacko in, so it was just us. We heard the shutters come down out front and watched as the manager walked around to the back and got into his car. He drove off. It was 5.05 p.m. We were ready.

'I've been up before,' said Chris, 'and checked out the door at the top of the fire escape. So ...'

I knew what was coming. Now it's my turn.

'... now it's your turn.'

It was pointless trying to complain and argue my way out of it. Not that I didn't want to show myself to be a true coward through and through – I think deep down we all knew the score on that front – but when it came to Chris, arguing was pointless; he just stared at you as if you'd starting talking Japanese. Decisions were made and stuck to, and poncing around with words just wasn't part of Chris's vocabulary.

Bearing in mind that Chris was pushing me to do the dirty work, I was nicely surprised to turn around halfway up the stairs and instead of seeing him smirking at the bottom, find him right behind me on the way up. It felt good to know that he had been up there already and fiddled about with the door (at least he'd done some of the groundwork), but then again I felt a short-lived stab of anger that he was stealing my glory. As far as I could tell, this was my party and I didn't want anyone getting in the way of the glory.

But the anger soon got swamped by the return of the nerves. I was right up at the door, and suddenly ripping off a high-street electrical retailer in broad daylight felt a whole lot less glamorous. The door was one of those that obviously had a push-down bar on the inside, and I could see how easy it would be to prise it apart just enough to see whatever wires were running across on the other side.

Chris pushed me out of the way and pulled out a foot-long screwdriver from his jacket. Wedging it in the gap where the two doors met, he managed to sort me out with a gap just large enough to get a couple of skinny fingers through.

'All you've got to do is cut that wire,' he helpfully informed me. I looked.

'But there's only one wire. There are supposed to be two.' Why I thought there had to be two I'm not sure, but in my mind I was prepared for a two-wire alarm system. I was confident approaching the old paired-up alarm, but singles ... now that was a different story.

'I can't do it,' I whispered, hoping that he wouldn't question me as to why the job was off. We could be home in front of the telly in 10 minutes. Chris didn't look convinced.

'I can't do it because I haven't got any wire cutters.' Ha! I'm a genius, me!

'Good job I brought these,' said Chris, handing over a pair of yellow-gripped cutters. Bastard.

Now Chris wasn't stupid, or at least not as stupid as I was. He'd set it up from way back at the bottom of the steps and I was firmly in the doing-the-cutting seat. Before I could complain he shot through a list of reasons why I should be doing the deed. I didn't really hear them either, as it was his eyes that told me this was the way that things were going to be. Gripping each arm of the cutters between my thumb and forefinger I held them in position, the blades pausing either side of the wire. I wondered whether this was the right wire to cut, but since there was only that one around, it must have been correct. I squeezed the cutters together.

Of course the alarm went off. It sounded like a spaceship landing as the bells were ringing, lights were flashing and some horrible screeching noise was banging out a dirty-sounding 4/4 beat. Chris and I ran back down the fire escape to be greeted by what wasn't exactly a welcome sight: two uniformed coppers legging it towards us over the rubble.

I think I would have had a better chance of escaping had I not been spontaneously sick. It had all got too much for me and there was nothing that I could really do. I stood there, dazed, puke dripping from my mouth, feeling as though the end of the world was about to land on me. Chris had made a run for it but hadn't got much further than I had before he was caught by the other copper. We were taken down to the police station, and I got my first taste of real trouble.

'I'm dead ... I'm dead ... I'm dead ... I'm going to prison and then I'm really going to be dead ... they're going to know all about the cars and the rest of it ... they're going to show me pictures of myself torching a motor and they'll make me confess to it all ... and they'll probably try and pin some other stuff on me too; some high-profile cases that have been gathering the dust of the unsolved ... I'll be 40 by the time I see the sun again ... I'm dead.'

I'd expected them to take things a bit more seriously, or at least to get angry with me, but these coppers had obviously seen it all before. As far as they were concerned I was just another nuisance, another potential thief in the making, and they just couldn't be bothered. They were sick of pulling these little scallies in, especially the ones who couldn't even rob properly, and after a time in the cells they gave us our cautions. My mum had come down by then, and if I thought she was going to be as unimpressed by my behaviour as the police I was wrong. She went ballistic.

I got back home to the biggest telling-off of my life. Things seemed to be making sense as she began to figure out that her little lad wasn't quite the cherub she'd taken him for until now. She brought up a whole load of stuff that I thought I'd got away with, like the mysterious disappearance of her record collection which I'd sold for a couple of packs of fags. She told me I wasn't going out of my room for a week, that I was never to see Chris again and all that. In the middle of the storm, with her shouting and all that, I realized something: what did it matter? If I had to stay in all day, so much the better, at least I could catch up on my sleep and be ready for the night back out with my mates. If I got caught by the police again, so what? It just didn't seem to be a big deal at the time.

And so I finished my first wave of scally education, passing with flying colours. As any young 'un who likes to flirt with trouble knows, you'll get nowhere if the punishments mean anything. I'd had my vaccinations and for a few years at least I'd be safe from harm. Anyway, mum was doin' my head in and it was high time I got out there and had what I thought was some more fun.

And fun naturally meant illegal. Whatever it was, as long as someone would at least tell us off for it, we'd give it a go. Children are supposed to like sweet shops, aren't they? Well, for me and Vinny, the sweet shop of life was open for business and we were planning on trying out the full product range.

Looking back now, all that sounds like the childish nonsense that it is. Living life to the max, I thought, meant taking as much as I could for myself, and it didn't matter what sort of experiences I took, or where they came from. I ended up leaving a bit of a trail of cack behind me; you know the sort of thing, relationships where I wasn't exactly on anything like my best behaviour, using people and then shipping out. Not good. But I can't deny there were laughs along the way, and me and Vinny set about having some top ones over the years. There were others in on them too, and Dennis and Darren Betts were two of the best to have around. Dennis plays rugby for Wigan now, and he always was a bit useful if things got physical. Which they did. Often.

Now, none of you are going to be surprised that our first acid trip was a bit of an adventure. I've yet to meet a tripper who can't say the same (except the ones in mental institutions), but all the same, if you'll indulge me for just a few minutes it'd be nice.

It was New Year's Eve 1980. Being the fully grown up 12-year-olds that we were, me and Vinny decided to celebrate in style, doing our bit to add to the local colour that always makes Wythenshawe New Years a spectacle to rival many of the cultural greats around the world. Gone were the days of sitting around watching the telly count us in; now it was time to join in for ourselves. And because we were so grown up and mature, we decided to do something different for a change and actually pay for our gear. OK, so it may have been out of a tenner that I nicked from me old man, but I felt I'd at least made the effort.

19

I'd not been that much into drinking really, but Vinny was determined that we got bladdered and stayed over at his sister's flat down the road. I wasn't arguing, and we squeaked our way to the local 7-11 to get our provisions in. One two-litre bottle of cider and half a bottle of vodka. Each. 'After all,' Vinny told me as we left the shop, 'it only happens once a year, right?'

Seven-ten p.m. and it was time to get the party going. The location for our celebrations was something special, just inside the gates of our own primary school. Somehow we both managed to get through the cider, although I must have tipped half of mine away while Vinny wasn't looking, and then we started on the voddy. It was the worst taste I'd ever had, but of course, there was no way I was telling Vinny that. He may have done better on the cider, but he was spluttering and spitting away like a rabid dog now we'd moved on to the real man's stuff. I made myself as brave as I could and drank.

So I woke up. I was lying down, that much I could tell, but it was a lot noisier than it had been in the school. I could hear cars and the odd voice. They were tutting away and muttering about what a terrible thing it was to see. I sat up and worked out where I was. I'd come about 100 yards from the school and was lying by Greenbrow Road, a main road that ran through Wythenshawe. I was covered in puke and only had one thought in my mind: home. I managed to make my way back and met my mum inside.

'What's going on?' she asked.

Summoning up all the dignity in my body and trying to look like a cross between Face out of the A Team and Roger Moore, I explained I'd just had a little drink with Vinny, that it had been a good night and that I'd see her in the morning.

'A good night? It's only eight o'clock.'

I was too busy peeling off my clothes as I walked up the stairs. I got into bed and drifted. The room spun but at least I was warm and lying on something soft.

Crime# Crime

Next thing I knew I was shaking. I'd woken myself up with it and for a moment worried that I was having some kind of fit. I opened my eyes and saw Vinny, can in hand, grinning at me like he'd just won the pools.

'Comeonshittead itsonlynineoclock.'

He dragged me out of bed and tried to force some clothes on me. But there was no way I was having any of it and I wound up asleep on the floor while he was chucking my undies at me. Eventually he gave up and saw the New Year in on his own.

The next day Vinny came round. I don't know how he did it, but he was still walking, talking and smiling. He must have still been bladdered, and this time I couldn't get rid of him. We'd missed the chance to go and stay with his sister and he wasn't going to let an opportunity like that pass him by again. He must have known something I didn't as he was dead keen to get over there, and not being in much of a state to do anything other than follow behind, I followed behind.

We got there and saw Sally with a sheet of trips in front of her. Naturally we didn't know they were trips, and for one terrible moment Vinny thought his sister had got big time into stamp collecting.

'Oh, don't mind, lads. Just have one of these,' she said as she passed a couple of titchy little bits of paper over to us. She was about 22 or 23, and it wasn't as if she was some kind of evil drug pusher. She just wanted her little brother and his mate to have a laugh.

We took half each and went outside to sit on the stairs. Now Vinny always made me laugh anyway, and whenever we were hanging out he'd get on with a few gags, telling stories he'd heard about people or taking the mick out of others. So at first nothing was different; Vinny was chatting and I was laughing. But as the hour moved on I started laughing harder and harder as Vinny seemed to have taken some kind of comedy steroids. He was on fire and my stomach was in serious pain.

21

It was after a while that we realized this wasn't quite normal. The laughing was still there but it felt as if I was watching myself from behind a two-way mirror. I could step back, look at what I was doing and how I was behaving while my body carried on without me. It was as if my whole self had shrunk into a tiny little me and the two mes were attached just at the eyeballs. We both agreed that it felt a bit weird and Vinny said he wanted to go and have a lie down. I knew what he meant so we went back into the flat and got into his sister's bed, him at one end and me at the other.

'You all right, mate?'

'Yeah. Are you?'

'Yeah.'

Silence.

'Do you feel a bit weird, mate?'

'Yeah. Do you?'

'Yeah.'

Silence.

'You all right, mate?'

'Yeah. Are you?'

'Yeah.'

It went on for ages. Eventually we both lifted our heads up at the same time, slowly craning them forward to look down the other end of the bed. He saw what I saw, a head that was somewhere it wasn't supposed to be, floating.

'Vinny.'

'Yes, mate.'

'There's someone at the end of me bed.'

'There's someone at the end of my one too.'

We both jumped out of bed and were freaked. It was time to get back outside, to get some fresh air and away from this strange room with the floating heads. It was dark outside, and we were walking along carrying on our crap conversation about how it felt, when we saw a group of lads that we kind of knew walking towards us. For some reason we decided that we mustn't let them know that we were tripping, but once we stopped it didn't take long for one of them to suss it out, owing to the fact that we were still talking rubbish.

I was talking to Pez while another was standing off to one side.

'D'you wanna nut?' said the bloke at the side.

'Yeah,' I said as I looked round. He was eating a bag of nuts but he wasn't looking my way at all and the bag was not being held out. So I carried on my conversation with Pez.

'D'you wanna nut?'

I did want a nut and I turned round to put my hand in the bag, but again it wasn't being held out. Again he was talking to another lad, not looking at me, but this time I was definitely convinced that I'd heard him offer me a nut. But why did he offer me a nut and then not let me take one? Pez started talking, and then nut-man asked again,

'D'you wanna nut?'

I looked and this time the bag was out, but as soon as I went to grab a nut he pulled it back. He started laughing and Vinny and I looked at each other and legged it, with the whole load of them shouting 'D'you wanna nut?' after us. Funnily enough, I never really did get into acid that much.

Nut. Nut. D'you wanna nut? Do I? A nut? Do I? Did he say that? I'm lying in my bed, face down. My eyes are open. Walking home the grass was purple and the sky was green. I found an apple. I called it My Happy Apple and as long as I held it safe my mind was safe too. It was a nice apple, perfect and all that. I felt happier with it and that was good. Until Vinny took a bite out of it. He told me he was hungry but I don't think I believe him. I think he knew how important My Happy Apple was to me. So that's why I'm lying here with my eyes open. I can see little animals running over my arms but I'm not worried about them. I reckon they'll get tired and go to sleep soon too. But I'm wondering about the drugs. Have they hurt me? Will I always be seeing things from out the corner of my eyes from now on?

Vinny came back with me and sat on the floor playing with his shoelaces. Then he went. I'm looking around myself now and for some reason I'm wondering what's up with my room. It's not a big room – just long enough for a bed and a wardrobe down one side and a cupboard on the other near the door – and it always looks quite long and thin to me. But not tonight. Not now. I'm sat up now, looking about me, and I'm convinced that the room looks a lot wider and shorter than usual. Convinced of it. Absolutely no doubt about it; this is a different room. OK. OK. I can handle that. Although ... in fact, I would even have to go so far as to say that this isn't my room. So that's a nice little thought to tide me over, isn't it? I'm in a room but it's not my room. Great. But look, there's all my gear thrown about the room, just how I remember leaving it earlier. There's my towel, my football, my bag, there are my posters, my trousers and my T-shirts. So – and it's all starting to get a bit too weird now – I'm thinking, 'If this doesn't look like my room but it's full of my stuff ... who am I?' Does that make me some kind of an impostor, a plant, a double, a dummy? Has someone switched me with the real me and I've only just realized? My body is Cameron Dante, surrounded by his stuff, but the mind is someone else entirely. So what does that mean?

GLUE

Amanda Jenkins was the city bike. Me and Vinny were sat around Chris's house one day when she knocked on the door. Chris told us that he was just going upstairs with her, and being 12, Vinny and I looked confused. They went up and we got back to watching the telly.

'Go on then. You do her.'

Chris was standing in the doorway doing his zip up and looking at me. The penny dropped. I shuddered.

'Arright, I'll do 'er then,' I said, shuffling off, hoping I'd said the right thing.

Now I'd always quite liked Amanda Jenkins. I don't mean that I ever fancied her, it's just that she seemed like a laugh. Actually I did fancy her, I thought she was sexy and sophisticated, a real woman, but as I walked up the stairs I just started to feel nervous.

She was sat on top of the stairs. She knew what she was there for, she knew what I was there for and I had some kind of idea about what I was supposed to be doing, but I bottled it.

'Arright Amanda. Howsitgoing?'

'Arright Cam.'

25

Too much time passed during which I played through all the different types of move I could make to see if they might work.

'So then. Do you want me to do you?'

Nah.

'Chris reckons we'd be good together and I love you, Amanda Jenkins.'

Too much of a mouthful.

How about just unzipping my flies and hoping she gets the hint?

We chatted for about half an hour, and that was it. She didn't get the hint. Of course Chris ripped it out of me, calling me a poof and all that for the rest of the afternoon. I was not happy, so it's hardly surprising that when he pulled out a tub of Evostik later on, I was game on. I may not have been sure about sex, but what with me being a full-time smoker, I considered myself an expert in the theory of drug taking. I'd been taking an interest in it all for months, and I'd built up an impressive bank of knowledge inside my tiny head. I knew that glue made you feel like Superman and that if you breathed enough in you'd be able to fly. Something like that anyway.

Out in the back garden he'd poured some from the tub into a carrier bag, showed me how to get a good wafting action going and invited me to get on with it. I was in a bit of a state even before I got down to business, but as the fumes began to take effect my mind shifted into another gear. It was a headrush unlike any I'd ever had before. It was all those times of spinning till I made myself dizzy and fell over rolled into one, put into a biscuit tin and thrown into a cement mixer. My mind was a lead weight – directing my own thoughts was way too much to ask of it – but images and ideas flashed in and out of it at hurricane speed. I was floating, that much was true, but I didn't feel anything like Superman. At least I hoped he didn't feel like this all the time.

26

Glue

I know that Amanda grabbed my hand and took me upstairs, but apart from that the rest of the afternoon is a blur. That's when I lost my virginity, so I'm told, but I'm buggered if I can remember it.

Looking back the real highlight of the day seemed to be the glue. The sex was something that I'd got out of the way, but the glue, well, that seemed like something special. Me, Vinny and Chris soon developed a taste for the stuff and settled down to regular sessions. It was cheap, although of course we never paid for it. Hardware stores hadn't sussed out what was going on by that point, and the silver tin with the red writing and shining sun in the background was always within easy reach. For the ones who did catch the thieves I suppose they must have thought that us young folk had rediscovered a passion for model-making. How sweet.

The three of us knew that it wasn't something to be shouted about either. We'd do it in the garden if we had to, but usually we'd take our equipment with us down to the railway tracks. Not only did it mean that we could get on with the job uninterrupted, but we were guaranteed plenty of space and time for the 'trip', if you could call it that. Even in my most desperate state years later, when there'd be no Es, coke, alcohol or smack about, I'd never go back to glue. It was the lowest high I've ever had, and I don't think I've ever been tempted since we packed it in.

But before we get too far down that road, there were a few months when glue was still our thing. The rush was the thing, and we were always keen to go higher. We'd try different brands and that, but it was to Evo that we always returned. If there was any other way of taking it I'd have tried it too, and having seen some film where people snorted coke I got Vinny to guinea-pig the nasal technique. His nose wasn't good for much for quite a while after that. Anyway, as I said, we'd be down there on the railway tracks. They weren't in use any more and there was a huge patch of waste land surrounding our laboratory. They were building the M602 nearby and the whole place was deserted. They were building high barriers to keep some of the future traffic noise from the estate, and just a stone's throw from the building work were three deserted houses. They were notorious for all sorts of weird stuff going on: all the usual drug taking and dealing, mixed in with the weird blokes who looked at you funny and always looked as though they were thirsty. We'd run away from them on the rare occasion that they turned up, but for the most part we were guaranteed a bit of peace and quiet for the duration. I don't know, perhaps even perverts have standards.

Well, I say we had peace and quiet, but there was all this construction work going on all the time. On one of our first times down there I was leaning against a wall, huffing it all up into my lungs, when the strangest feeling came over me, and not the sort of strange feeling I'd already come to expect. I felt myself merging in with the wall, as if I was actually becoming a part of it. The noise of the workmen seemed to get louder until my mind was obsessed with a single thought: that somehow the motorway was finished and I was still trapped in the wall. They'd built me in and in my mind I could see all the cars driving by, with none of them stopping to help me. I was screaming as loud as I could but no one was stopping. Years passed by and I was going nowhere. But then, as trips often seem to do for me, things changed and I found my mind getting shafted by the most horrific revelation about what life was actually all about: I *knew* then that the entire world was one big construction site, a building created by others, with humans just as much a part of it as the roads and houses. There was no such thing as personality, no such thing as freedom or individuality. We were all slaves, all trapped and there was no escape. I was a lot of fun to be around in those days.

They might have been bad, but these experiences never really put me off. It's always the way though, isn't it? The nightmares become the stories, the moments of panic become the jokes.

Glue

There were strange feelings lurking at the back of my mind whenever I was off my head and getting into a state. At least it wasn't boring and I'd get a few stories out of it, I'd sometimes think. Other times – and this is when I was older – I'd feel as though I was getting deeper into myself, getting closer towards some type of (less paranoid) revelation. What that revelation was I never found out, or not on acid at least. By the time ecstasy and coke came my way I'd had enough of all this looking in on myself. I wanted to feel fantastic, not sit around thinking about construction conspiracies.

One time the three of us had made our way down to the railway and were having a friendly chat in between bags. As I came up on the glue one of my more usual trips emerged. I'd managed to disappear into thin air and was surrounded by stars and moons. It was all very pleasant, or it was until I realized that I needed to go for a dump. Badly. I made my way out of sight of Vinny and Chris and squatted down against a wall. Ah. Sweet relief.

'POLICE!' I heard someone shout.

I panicked. I threw my bag down and legged it as fast as I could across the rubble. I'd only had time to pull my trousers a little way up and after a few steps they were back round my ankles. I fell over and landed on a pile of old bricks, cutting up my arms and legs in the process. I looked around to see Chris and Vinny staring out at me, both frozen still with their bags halfway up to their mouths.

'What you doing?' I shouted. 'Get out of here!'

'And why would we want to do that, Cam?' asked Chris.

'Because of the police,' I shouted back, struggling to pull my keks back up and making a mental note to have a chat with Chris about the fact that the glue seemed to be taking its toll on his powers of observation.

'What police? We just thought you was tripping,' Chris said, and they both went back to huffing the fumes from out of their bags.

By the time I was approaching 13 I was nicely hooked on the stuff. When a tub was empty I'd think about nothing other than where the next one was coming from, and when a new one came my way, my next thought would be when I was going to crack it open. I was on it almost every day and I'd long since had the tell-tale spots all around my mouth.

One day I woke up and didn't fancy waiting all that time till the three of us went out, so, knowing my mum was downstairs, I decided to have a quick blast indoors. I thought I'd be clever and tuck myself away somewhere for the duration, so I went and hid in the bottom of the airing cupboard. All the neatly pressed sheets were on the shelves above me and there I was at the bottom, merrily filling my lungs with as much premium-grade adhesive as possible. Of course, just when I'd got settled in the door opened and my mum was standing there with a fresh batch of sheets. She didn't see me as she was putting them away, but as she was closing the door she looked down, saw me and screamed.

Now as far as I was concerned I'd become an adult. I'd left the ways of my parents and was writing this adventure for myself. I didn't mind getting in trouble – with them or the police – and I certainly didn't care about school or anything like that. But I never hated my parents. So I was kind of torn during the fallout from this discovery. Mum went mad, obviously upset and worried for me, and struggling with the final bit of evidence that her lad was no longer just sweet and innocent. She knew that Chris had been a bad influence, but seeing me on the glue on my own must have made her think twice about how much I was just a victim of one bloke's persuasive powers. She could no longer hide behind the comfort of blaming it all on Chris, imagining that I only ever got up to bad stuff with one arm twisted behind my back. No, from this point on she had to face up to the fact that this scally behaviour was something I was choosing for myself. Of course, looking back it's obvious that there was a big game of follow the leader being played with Chris and us, and I think I knew it even back then. But when it came to arguing it out with my mum I was up for making a stand myself. The arguments went on for a long time. Never with my dad, though. He was always somewhere just out of shot whenever it came to discussions about my wicked ways, leaving his wife to lead the attack.

It didn't turn me off Chris though. I don't think I ever really thought he was many leagues beyond me and Vinny, but he was mad enough to command a fair bit of respect from each of us. Dean and Wacko were still around, but they were never quite so into the glue. They'd be there when we were just hanging about, there when we did the odd car or whatever, but there was – and I'm sorry to chuck a pun like this – something of a bond between Vinny, me and Chris.

I think it was the fact that we were a tight little unit that eventually caught the attention of some of the local families. Now don't think I've come over all Godfather here, but in Manchester the crime tends to be run by families, and back then, they all lived local. Each family would have their own speciality – drugs, robbing shops, lending money and the like – and their own little patch. Me and Chris and Vinny were, as I said, still doing the odd car and stuff, and we soon got talking with some of these influential people. It didn't take long to work out that they were taking more than just a sentimental interest in us, and they wanted more than just to be able to pass a few tricks on to the new blood. Being the 13-year-old scallies that we were, we were decidedly useful. If we got caught by the police we wouldn't go down, and could take more risks than other, older blokes. What's more, we were cheap.

Saying that it was we who got in with this new group isn't exactly true. It was Vinny and me who got the promotion, leaving Chris behind. We'd all been hanging out together for a long time, but I seriously think that the glue was taking its toll on him far more than it was on us. Chris started to flip a bit, skipping between mad ideas every few hours. One minute he'd be trying to set fire to cats and the next he'd be announcing a new competition to see which one of our little lot was the hardest. I remember that particular test well, as Chris stood up, stuck his chin out and told Vinny to take a free punch. He did, but not with quite enough passion. He'd failed to take Chris's right arm out of action, and Vinny's face became the rapid owner of a look of pure fear as Chris shook his head and grinned a wicked grin.

'My turn,' he said, lining up for a free shot.

Of course he won. Vinny was spitting blood for the rest of the afternoon, and despite the fact that Chris was virtually begging him to carry on, offering him free shots with any tool Vinny fancied, we knew things were turning odd. So I suppose it's not surprising that when someone more exciting but less insane came along, Vinny and I were well up for moving on.

There was one particular family that I got on best with. The Dukes were great, and their youngest – Darren – became a good friend, even though he was a few years older than me. Immediately I noticed something different: whenever someone asked me who I knocked about with and I told them it was Darren Duke, I got respect. When I used to be in the position of saying that it was Chris that I was hanging about with, the reply was always a blank look and the words 'Chris who?' Now things were different. Even though Darren had done no more than Chris when it came to crime, the family name was enough on its own due to the activities of some of the clan.

The family were your typical British bulldog types. Of a Saturday night the whole lot of them would be off down The Mariner on Aytoun Street. Darren and I would be sat out the front and from time to time someone would bring us out a couple of pints of lager and a few crisps. It was heaven and we loved every minute of it. We'd be getting bladdered on our own out there, chatting up the ladies and making ourselves look hard and scaring the kids who walked by. The evening would always end the same too, with chairs flying out of the door and fights spilling out onto the street. It was all a laugh, all part of Wythenshawe living. Pubs weren't there for quiet drinks and quizzes, they were there so that you could get wrecked and some decent violence could kick off.

But while I was feeling like I had been adopted into the family, Darren was feeling different. He was the youngest and was kind of in the shadow of his brothers. They were out doing the stuff already – armed robberies and all that – but I never got the feeling that Darren wanted to follow in their footsteps.

'It's just not me,' he told me once.

Now I'm not going to lie and make out that he was some sensitive, arty type who just wanted to break away from the family life of crime and write tender poetry in Provence. Darren liked a good scrap and he wasn't afraid of nicking the odd bit of kit to keep himself in ready cash. It's just that he wasn't 100 per cent with it all. He didn't want the risk and the worry that came with the life of a medium-sized crim; for him it just got in the way and failed to be outweighed by the adrenaline buzz of a crime mid-execution. Darren was far more your homely type, far more the kind of bloke who'd be happy pushing a pram and enjoying life with the family. Come to think of it, that's exactly how it ended up, but not quite as smoothly as you might think.

Even though Darren was hardly making a name for himself as the latest contender for the Manchester Psycho throne, the relevant members of the Duke family were still holding their own on the circuit. Their crime levels were high enough and they had plenty of respect from the likes of the Coxes. There were other big crime families in the area at the time too, and looking back now I'm surprised that there never seemed to be much aggro between them. These families simply weren't up for fighting against each other. There was a strong sense of unity between them, and jobs, drugs and information would often get passed around between them. The real fight was between the Wythenshawe families and people from other areas like Moss Side and Salford.

But it wasn't just the families who were up for it against Moss Side, the rest of us scallies were keen to wave the Wythenshawe flag too. That's why when the National Front came recruiting round our way, they always got a good response. All they had to do was to heat up the old lies about the black and Asian communities in Moss Side taking our jobs and we'd be with them like a shot. It's stupid and it's embarrassing to look back on it now, but I can remember getting involved when the NF arranged a march in Wythenshawe. I'd be there with my placard, shouting the racist abuse, following behind the nasty-looking skinheads who always looked to me like they were chewing wasps. We'd get warmed up in the safety of the mostly white Wythenshawe, but eventually we would make our way to the edge of town where Moss Side began. It would all kick off there and then and the families would be down the front, doing it large and giving it all the hatred and violence they could. It was all part of the act.

It's funny that I got on so well with this idea of families who were in charge, as I've always hated authority. I suppose we all do in our way, but for as long as I can remember, whenever anyone has told me to do something I've had a burning desire to do the exact opposite. This was never more of an issue than when I was at school. I was wagging it all the time, and I totally blew my education. From day one I told myself there was nothing in there that I needed to learn. As far as I was concerned I was going to be a pop star, and maths, English and woodwork weren't going to be of much use to me on *Top of the Pops*.

Glue

My dad hadn't exactly enjoyed school either, although he had it much worse than I did. While my school was run by a few well-meaning but out-of-touch teachers, my dad's was ruled by a sadistic bunch called the Christian Brothers. Each had a leather strap hanging out of the back of their habit and they weren't shy of using them. My dad says that any little thing they did wrong was punished immediately by a few whacks from the strap. He's an intelligent man, my dad, a real thinker, but he switched off at school. My mum was the same, taught by nuns but leaving at the end without any real respect for the place. For both of them what they were taught at school had no relation to what they did for work, and as far as I was concerned, things weren't going to be any different for me either. And why should they? At the time it might have been more about rebellion and the fact that I hated Drennan, but now it seems obvious that I was never going to get on with school. It wasn't just my parents' views either; wherever I looked I could see people who were doing well without any help at all from school, I could see people who had studied hard and put their faith in the system only to get nothing in return. There were nothing more than the simple options; crime, the dole or having your soul destroyed by some meaningless job. School wasn't a knight in shining armour; it was an impotent irrelevancy.

To add to the troubles, my school was in a bit of a state, a real Catch-22. They were the fag end of the local education system, but for some reason the staff were fighting hard to keep it open. It must have been rough for them with little scallies like me kicking it all back in their face, knowing that they really were the last ones who gave a toss about me, but they carried on. That's why, despite my near-constant suspensions, I never got expelled. Hardly anyone ever did from Cathedral Roman Catholic, as I guess now that the more they expelled the more they were admitting failure. But the end was inevitable, as the year after I left they closed the school down. I heard the teachers had been putting up a real fight for years.

Vinny and I had known not to push it too far though, and while we wagged it most days, we'd often make an effort to go in for morning registration to get the mark by our name. But once that first bell rang, we were out. It showed too, when the time came to sit our CSEs. Neither of us had thought about revision – we probably would have had enough trouble spelling it – and we would just turn up to the exams and write something if we could think of an answer. There were no nerves, no panics, no mad rushes to get as much written down as possible as the final minutes ticked away. Like I say, it wasn't going to be much use to me as a pop star, so why waste the effort?

But I did have a go at making something of my life. When I left school at 16 I signed up for a place on a YTS scheme. It was supposed to be training me for a future career, but all I learnt from six weeks at William Cox in Trafford Park was how to look for dog ends while sweeping the floor and how the entire shop floor liked their tea. It was a good deal for them, all I cost was £26.50 per week, and it gave the bosses an opportunity to feel like they were doing me some massive favour.

'Oh yes,' they'd say as I swept the floor for the sixteenth time that day, 'good brushwork always comes in handy. You'll never know when you'll need to use a broom.'

I knew exactly when I would need to use a broom, and it was when I showed them where to stick it. But I hung on for a little while, keeping patient as I gave the system one opportunity to prove itself to me. And it wasn't all bad either, as every afternoon there was a little bit of a highlight as I was sent off down the bookies with all the bets for the workers. Sometimes I'd have three or four hundred quid in my pocket, and it was always good taking back the winnings. There was one bloke who did way better than the rest, and he always seemed to be picking the winners. I was too young to bet myself, but every so often he'd put a quid on for me and I'd end up doubling my wages for the week.

I never got into the gambling, though. My dad has always liked a flutter, but it's never been a big deal for him. My brother on the other hand, well, that's a different story. He's doing nicely for himself now, but he nearly lost it all before, and all because of the casinos. While it was fun getting a little extra on top of the YTS wage, I was earning so little that I didn't dare risk throwing it away. I still feel the same, that the money you've grafted for is too precious just to chuck away. Even back then in my early teenage years I was preferring to put what spare cash I had into miniature investment schemes. I'm not talking banks and stuff here, you understand, but the sort of scally ideas that take cash, balls and no one poking their nose in.

I'm not living like this. If this is the way my life is going to be, I'm not taking it. They can forget jobs and all that. I'm making my own way from now on in. No more trying to play by the rules. I'm making my own path. But who am I trying to fool, eh? Am I so unique, so puffed up and talented that I can make it big on my own?

That's not the point. I know the routine, those arguments why I should bother. Be sensible, Dante. You need a trade. You need something to fall back on. Trouble is, there is nothing to fall back on. You want proof? Look at the miners on TV. Remember those riots a year ago? It's all part of the same reaction.

But enough of all that grand stuff; I'm not in it for the making of statements or the fighting of causes. I'm out to sort myself out, and that's as far as it goes. A little bit selfish for one so young? Too much of a Me First attitude? Yeah. What else is there to believe in?

LINO

It all started with The Rock Steady Crew. Malcolm McLaren brought them over and plastered them all over *Top of the Pops* some time around 1985, but of course, me and Darren knew the score already. We'd been watching home videos from New York for months, buying them off a mate of a mate who had a brother out there. By the time it went massive over here, there were already loads of us all over Manchester who were regularly doing battle on a little patch of lino.

'Buffalo Girls'. 'Breaker's Revenge'. 'Wicki Wicki Wicki Wicki'. 'Breakdance Electric Boogie'. They were all the big tunes, and it was to this last one by The Westside Mob that me, Darren and a guy called Dominic did our routines. Darren was more into the security side of things, come to think of it, as his skills on the mat were never as good as his talent with a headbutt and a fist. Perhaps this is why I got into it. I'd never been much of a fighter but I wanted respect, and from all those early videos it was plain to see that breakdancing was the ultimate way of doing battle. You didn't get hurt and it didn't drag on too long. You came out with your looks, got to look cool and would probably end up with loads of girls after you. It was my idea of heaven.

I can't remember how I met Dominic, I think he was just a mate from around the Precinct, but as it is when you're young, we threw ourselves into the breakdancing with all our passion. Within a couple of weeks we felt like brothers who'd been body-popping for years.

The first move we sussed was the Runaround. It took a while to get it right, but eventually the old leg was spinning nicely around underneath as I was crouched down on the ground. I liked the gymnastic side of things, and eventually I moved on to Windmills and Headspins. Dominic was always much more of a bodypopper, so between the two of us we had the basics covered.

Neither of us was shy, so within a few weeks of starting we regularly went down Wythenshawe market and did an hour's worth of routines. Sometimes we'd get as much as £40 in the cap, which for a couple of 14-year-olds was never a bad thing. Doing it was also a good way of getting your name about and meeting other people into the same thing, and it was through it that I heard about a new crew who were starting up. Dominic and I called ourselves Double Trouble, but this new lot had a much better name: Street Justice. Nice. There were quite a few of them in it already – the leader, a guy called Lil, had been doing the rounds recruiting people for a while – and they asked me to join. It was a bit of a bittersweet pill as they wanted me but not Dominic (they had a better bodypopper already). I never was big on loyalty back in those days, so I bailed out on my mate and joined up.

This world of crews was a new thing to me. Instead of it being just two of us I was now one of eight, each one having their own speciality. I was doing well on my Windmills, so that's what I stayed doing, but other guys were helping keep the whole spectrum covered. It was there that I met a guy called Rhino. He was an all right guy, and we got on well. He had this mad idea about doing stuff together, something he said that he'd seen at a circus when he was little. So we devised a whole routine made up of Spins, Windmills and the like, but with a nice little twist added: we'd be tied together at the leg. It wasn't like we were hand-cuffed or anything, and the rope had a good bit of length on it, but all the same it looked pretty decent, and got us that little bit more attention.

Joining up with Street Justice meant getting involved with battles against other crews. The nearest and biggest were the two Manchester-based ones: Broken Glass and Street Machine. They were both hot, much better than Street Justice, with some seriously talented individuals in them. Like I said, loyalty never was one of my strong points, so when they asked me and Rhino to join, we both jumped at the chance.

This was getting serious now. Instead of people that I vaguely knew, people who came from the same area and had similar backgrounds, I was travelling across Manchester, meeting a whole range of people. Before going down to join them for my first prac-tice I'd made sure that I'd gone on a special nicking spree with a top blagger called Benno. Together we'd been ripping off Manchester shops for months, always going for a better and better class of merchandise. We'd just moved up to Armani when the call from Street Machine came, so I was happy at last to have enough money to buy a new tracksuit. It was Fila, naturally.

The first practice stands out in my mind as a good one. I met Neverson, a massive black guy with huge afro and comb sticking out the back. He was a top guy, stoned out of his mind all the time, and it did me good to finally realize that all that NF stuff meant nothing to me at all. Then there was a young lad called Jason. He was a nice guy, one that I've got absolutely nothing bad to say about, apart from the fact that some of his early costumes in Take That were a bit rough. I can also remember finding out something very nice indeed: this thing paid. The crew had developed a good reputation for themselves and were getting loads of invites from around the country to go and have battles. They made a charge for an appearance and each member walked away with a little wad of notes for his trouble. I'd been thieving to get by, but knew this was a far better deal. The money may have been a bit less than I could get ripping off clothes stores but the risk was minimal and the buzz was definitely better. Legal earnings was something new too, and it seemed worth a shot.

One of the first battles was down in Nottingham against The Rock City Crew. Neverson was acting as our manager and had arranged for us all to wear denim jeans and jackets. We looked bad, with our names in graffiti down one arm and one leg. We had a little tag tied underneath our knee and our final trademark, kung fu slippers. We didn't go for any of those fat trainers – they were too cumbersome and heavy. With our slippers, though, we could just about fly.

We turned up and the atmosphere was buzzing. From outside you could hear 'Breaker's Revenge' ripping up the sound system and there were tons of people hanging around outside. We walked in, down through the middle of the venue in single file. I sneaked a look about me: it was massive and there must have been a few thousand people there. The buzz was top and I'd never been anywhere like it before. If I close my eyes I can still hear 'Pleasure Boys' by Visage tearing things up in there.

We cut through the crowd, went to the back of the stage and into our changing room. We'd just got in when a huge guy came to the door and shouted at us in his Nottinghamshire accent:

'OI! Are you lot Street Machine?'

We nodded.

'OUTSIDE, NOW!'

He was too big to argue with and we filed out. He lined us up against the wall and The Rock City Crew came out into the corridor. Taking each one in turn they got right up in our faces and started poking.

'So you think you're bad? You think you're going to beat us on our home ground?'

'Nah, mate,' we'd all splutter, trying not to get them any more angry. 'We're just here to do a bit of an exhibition.'

When they got to the end of the line they found Justin, the cheekiest, gobbiest little dude you've ever met. He can only have been about 13, and he was stuffed up with attitude. When they had a go at him he refused to cave in, and launched back at them in his squeaky little voice.

'Look man, I'd take every single one of you on. I'd take the whole lot of ya, one by one, and I'd still batter ya.'

The guy looked at him. Silence. Should I be ready to run? Then the whole crew burst out laughing.

As soon as they got on stage and we'd seen a bit of their routine, we were worried. They were terrible. The crowd was going wild at the slightest thing. One of their lot did a single Thomson Flare – one of those gymnastic moves where you sit off the ground with your hands holding you up and swing your legs around in a circle. This had us worried: our routine started with all eight of us doing three Thomsons at the same time. We were going to batter them on their home turf and it might not be too pretty.

Still, we weren't about to be put off, and we went and gave it all we had. The place went mental over the Thomsons. Rhino and I did our tied-up routine, then Jason did his bouncing cross-legged Windmills and all that. We creamed them, no question, and at the end we went down onto the dance floor and had individual battles with anyone who fancied a shot. We were knackered, but it put Street Machine's name on the map.

Lino

After the Rock City battle we got invited to do a whole load more. We did more travelling, and during that time my drug consumption went right down. I stopped using the glue and started getting into the idea of being a healthy breakdancer for a while. I liked how I felt too: as if I was in control again. At that age I had loads of energy no matter what I put my body through, so any benefits from laying off the gear were felt purely in the mental department. I'd wake up feeling reasonably happy, didn't have to worry about upsetting my mum and generally got into the idea of doing something with my days. I had a goal, a purpose, was getting some decent exercise and took a pride in my appearance. I was a model teenager. Sort of. Sickening, isn't it?

I'd also found myself a girlfriend. It had been a long time since the fumbles with Amanda Jenkins, and even though there had been one or two along the way, I was 15 now and felt like I was ready for something seriously adult. Trisha was someone I'd known for a while. She'd grown up round our way, and had hit the gossip headlines when she got pregnant when she was 14. Actually it wasn't her getting pregnant that got people talking, it was what her parents did to the father of the child. They went round to his house and battered the lad, his parents and the whole house itself. Trisha's parents were the protective kind, and they didn't mind showing it.

But I liked her. There was something appealing about going out with a girl who already had a kid. It meant she'd been there, she'd done that and she knew the score. She was just what a teenage lad wanted, and I was a happy lad. I'll not pretend that I was playing dad to the kid, and he was only a baby when we first got together, but it made me feel nice and grown up to go strolling down the precinct, pushing the pram with Trisha by my side.

There was another serious advantage too: she was going to get her own flat. Result. I was still at home at the time, and even

43

though I was gradually becoming more like the son my mum had wanted, the idea of being with a girl who had her own accommodation was too good to be true. The council were going to give her a place as soon as she turned 16, and the whole thing was a big buzz in the months leading up to it. But this all makes me sound a bit cynical. You know what it's like when you're a young 'un; little things matter. It didn't mean I liked her any less, but that's just about how deep things got between us.

There were other things on my mind. Breakdancing had pretty much become my life and it was the thing that came first. I even entered the 1986 UK Breakdancing Championships. I didn't think I had a chance but it was a way of getting a free ticket to see all those other greats from around the country coming to do their stuff.

The event was held at the Tropicana in Manchester, and was all done properly with sponsors, TV advertising and a panel of judges. There was a good buzz there on the night, and I was one of the last on. I'd seen some good people, and I'd only really worked out a basic routine in my head as I wasn't that confident. I was going to go from Windmill to Headspin, down to a bouncing Windmill into a funny thing I'd made up where my legs did the splits and my whole body twisted underneath. I went on, did my thing and came off, not really thinking that I'd done that well. I struggle to remember much more than the basics of it; how it felt's a bit of a blank to me. I guess my lack of confidence got transferred into a lack of nerves, making the whole thing just like another session on the practice mat. After I was finished there were two or three due to go on after me, but I wasn't that bothered about hanging around so I got my stuff and made my way out. A friend told me it had looked good, but I was on a bit of a downer and wouldn't hear of it. I was actually at the bottom of the stairs about to leave when this same friend came legging it down the stairs screaming that I'd won.

Lino

I was gobsmacked. I walked back in and the crowd were cheering. I remember the feelings then; the greatest buzz I'd ever experienced. I was a grinning madman as I stumbled back onto the dance floor, shook plenty of hands, grinned a bit more and wondered what had happened. Then I went home, back to normal. There was no one in – they were down the pub, so the UK Breakdancing Champion opened a can of beans, watched a bit of telly, smoked a spliff and went to bed. And that was that. It was all just too weird.

The bad thing about it all back in those days was that no one had really got their act together. These days promoters would be in there like a shot, ready to sign you up and help capitalize on your success, but back then it was a case of 'Well done, see ya at the next event.' I won, but it didn't really mean anything in terms of change. Don't get me wrong, I was dead chuffed, but it's not as if it changed my life.

I did get to go to the World Championships though. They were a month later in Monte Catini, Italy, and I went over with Benjy, the guy who'd won the Bodypopping Championship. I'd never been abroad before and was still only 15½, so I was made up. I met loads of people from around the world. It was definitely a step up from the Tropicana; there were national TV and press there, it was all nice and glitzy, kind of like a slimmed-down Eurovision Song Contest. With hip hop. And no Terry Wogan.

I came third at the end of it all, and it changed the way I felt about things. I realized that I was never going to be anywhere near as good as some of the others, and there really didn't seem to be much point in carrying on.

I suppose there were other reasons why I was feeling a bit down about stuff at the time. Things hadn't been going so well with Trisha. She'd moved into her flat and so had I, kind of, which was fun for a while, but what with me being off so much with Street

Machine, things soon became a bit tense. She could hardly go off around the country whenever she wanted, and it probably seemed unfair that I was doing it myself. She was young and so was I, but her baby was getting a bit older now and he needed her to act more like a mother than just a babysitter. She did it well, she was a good mother, but I was still stuck in my old rut. As far as I saw it I had my things to deal with and she had hers. It was best that we just get on with them, and so it's not surprising that the whole thing didn't have that long to last.

I'd noticed little things that started to bother me a bit. Darren had long since stopped being interested in breakdancing, but we were still good mates. We'd pull off a few scams here and there when they came up, but things were beginning to change between the two of us. Not much, but just a bit. I noticed that he'd be coming round the flat to see me, and often when I'd get in from a practice or whatever he'd already be there, waiting for me. He and Trisha had always got on as mates, and I didn't think much of it, but it still felt odd, as if I never quite knew where he'd pop up. I suppose I started to get a bit suspicious.

One night I was out with the crew down at the Apollo, doing something, I can't remember what. Anyway, we were supposed to be there till late – midnight or something like that – and I'd arranged to meet Darren back at the flat. For some reason the thing with the crew finished earlier, and I gave Darren a call back at his home to tell him to come round earlier. He wasn't there, but his brother didn't know where he was, although he thought he'd gone round to mine. It didn't seem right and I played the situation over in my mind all the way back. Obviously I jumped to a massive conclusion with no real evidence at all. As far as I could tell, Darren was a mate and screwing your mate's bird was definitely out of the question. He wouldn't do that, not to me. But things had been getting a little odd, and lately I'd seen him round the flat on his own with Trisha more often than I'd seen him at his own house. I got back and decided to wait outside for a bit, sitting down on the ground outside the first-floor flat, waiting to see if Darren was going to go in.

I must have sat there for half an hour when I saw a silhouette move across the bedroom window. I got up and walked closer, trying to get a better look. The figure walked back and I could tell it was Trisha, looking like she just had a towel wrapped around her.

'This is stupid,' I thought. 'I'm suspecting my own girlfriend when all that she's done is stay in and have a bath.'

It was getting cold and I told myself off for being so stupid and letting my mind run away with me, walked to the door and let myself in.

But I hadn't been so stupid. I walked to the bedroom and saw Trisha and Darren. They weren't at it or anything like that, but let's just say you could tell they hadn't been doing the crossword. I couldn't believe it. I'd never been betrayed like that before, and I could feel it over every inch of my flesh. My insides were churning and I stood there stunned. Darren, hard as he was, had nothing to say either, and Trisha was just looking down at the floor.

Darren and I had fought together, had good laughs together. We'd backed each other up and were always watching each other's backs when we were out. It was him I felt more betrayed by, not Trisha. I was still young then, and still put my mates first.

Like all mates I'd wondered before who would come off best if Darren and I ever fought each other. I'd always thought that Darren would win – he had it all going for him: madness, size, technique and loads more practice. But he was doing nothing. Anger came up inside of me and that was it. I flipped. Ran over to him, grabbed a lamp that had a big vase base, and laid into him with it. I didn't know what I was doing, just letting the rage take over. He was lying down on the floor by the bed and I was punching him as hard and as fast as I could. I was shouting at him and Trisha was screaming. The kid came out into the room crying, and she tried to calm him down.

It stopped as quickly as it started. I left the room, grabbed my stereo and got out, heading for my parents' house. By the time I got there my parents had gone to bed and I went in quietly, back to my room. I was staying there every once in a while, so I don't suppose my mum would have been surprised to hear me back. I lay on my bed and thought the night through. I replayed it all in my mind, chucking in different things I wished I'd said. I thought about what I'd done to Darren and what he might be doing now. That wasn't a good thought to have, as I imagined him battered, going back home and telling his brothers. I played it over again and again, trying to convince myself that he wouldn't be in much of a state, that it would only be a matter of a scratch and a couple of bruises, but I knew it must have been worse. I'd been so mad and he'd done nothing, barely even lifting his arms up to protect himself. He'd be in a state right now and there were no two ways about it. I went to sleep feeling sick with worry.

The next day came. It was a Saturday and it didn't take long for my mum to work out that something was wrong. I told her that Trisha and I had had a fight, I didn't want her to know it all. She muttered something about how she'd told me not to get involved with a girl who already had a baby. If you only knew, I thought.

I decided that the best thing to do would be to lie low for a bit, if only to give myself some time to think about what I should do next. I was watching TV with my dad in the afternoon when there was a knock at the door. Crap, I thought, and made my way back through to the kitchen when I heard my mum open the door. I stopped when I heard a voice that definitely wasn't one of Darren's brothers'. I looked back in and saw Trisha coming in with her parents. I remembered what they'd done to the bloke

48

who knocked her up and I wondered how they'd react if they knew the truth about their daughter. It didn't make sense that they were here, but they seemed keen to talk. Her dad spoke first.

'Your son,' he said, looking back and forth between my parents, 'has done something and ...'

Trisha stopped him. 'I'm pregnant,' she said, looking straight at me. She was smiling.

All the anger came back from last night. She'd said it in a way that was 100 per cent loaded and it made me suspect that what she meant was 'I've got you now, sunshine. Your life is mine.' I was livid. How could she? How did she have the face to come in here, to my parents' house, and say that after what I'd seen the night before? I had a mind to tell them all about it, but what if she was right? What if it was my kid? I wanted no more to do with her, but couldn't let a kid of mine grow up without my help. I was about to speak when I saw something out of the corner of my eye that made me stop. It was Trisha; she had bent down and seemed to be about to throw something at me. I saw what it was in time to turn my head away. She'd chucked one of those big glass pub ashtrays at me and it landed on the back of my head. It hurt like nothing else. My mum was screaming, going absolutely mental, but when I looked up I saw it wasn't me she was shouting down but Trisha's parents. It all kicked off for real, with Mum taking them all on, and Trisha's parents looking much bigger. But size isn't everything and they could tell she meant business. She wasn't scared of no one, my mum, and she was forcing them down the hall and out the front door. Seeing the look in her eyes they probably thought I was going to get a far worse battering from her than even they would have delivered, and they didn't put up much of a fight.

ASCENSION

I've come upstairs now, leaving Dad just sitting there quietly, still watching the telly. There's blood coming out the back of my head and I ought to go into the bathroom to sort myself out. But this is all too much for me. What about Darren's family coming for their revenge? Will they be round in the morning to pay me back for whatever went on back there? What about all this stuff with Trisha? What can I do? I'm thinking of options but nothing's working. I can't get back with Trisha. She might say that she wants me around but it's a trap, something to drag me down forever. Staying here's no good either. It'll only be a matter of time before someone comes here; Darren, Trisha, her family, my mum. What's the point in staying around and waiting for it all to happen to me? Even the breakdancing has lost some of its sparkle so it's not even as if I have anything to look forward to here. I'm trapped and it does not feel good. I can't go on with this. I'm 17 and I'm not supposed to have all this on my shoulders. I need a way out and I don't care how drastic it is.

RUCKSACK

Dover to Calais. Sounds simple, don't it, but I managed to make a meal out of it. I started out leaving Manchester within a couple of days of Trisha's parents coming round, and I was about as green as they come. I had a knackered old rucksack – one of those ones with a metal frame and orange fabric that managed to dig into my skin in the places where it had become frayed. I could have done without it really, not just because of the maximum irritation it caused me whenever I tried to hike merrily about, looking like a purposeful traveller, but because all I'd brought with me could have fitted in a carrier bag. I'd packed a couple of pairs of undies, a pair of socks and a couple of jumpers. Common sense – along with most other things that I later needed – had been left at home along with my mum and dad.

But at 17 I thought I had it made. I had £80 burning a hole in my back pocket and as far as I was concerned I was set. I figured the stash was probably enough to take me around the world, but as I was only headed for Spain I convinced myself that I could afford the odd luxury along the way.

ASCENSION

By the time I arrived at Dover I had just £25 left. What made it worse was that I'd hitched it down there too, so I really wasn't sure where the other £55 had gone. So much for travelling in the lap of luxury. But at least I'd managed to do something right: I'd got away from home, from the Manchester scallies and the grief that was surely coming my way had I stuck around. Down south in the land of tea rooms and London wide boys all that Manchester stuff seemed like a long way away, but not quite far enough. I'm not sure whether it was the prospect of them managing to track me down that kept me going or the desire to get as far away as possible from everything that reminded me of me. I wanted a fresh start and maybe somewhere deep down was a voice telling me that real fresh starts could only be made in foreign countries. Maybe I was desperate for adventure, to taste life to the max. Maybe it was fate, or maybe I was called there by some higher power.

Fruit machines, more like. I'd always wanted to go on a ferry: the chance of so many top distractions – the fruit machines, bevvies, cheap smokes as well as the chance to join twenty other people throwing up on deck – was something that I just couldn't pass up.

I wasn't sure if my £25 was gonna be enough to get me across, but somewhere I'd heard that you could always blag a free crossing from the truckers. As I wandered about the expanse of concrete where the lorries were waiting to board, I realized that for the first time I was almost excited. So far, the rides that had got me to Dover had been desperate attempts to get as far away as fast as possible. I'd come from Manchester to Bracknell with a salesman from Pontefract, a couple of students took me round to Enfield and a bona fide Essex boy Escorted me on down to within a few miles of Dover. Climbing up into the cab with Jim – a man towing 200 tons of Scottish salmon over to Luxembourg – was the first time that I felt excited. I was about to put a serious barrier between me and the past and it felt good.

Rucksack

The ride over on the boat saw me strutting about as if I were on the QE2. I sampled the fine lager in the bar, gambled decadently on the fruity and tried not to fall over as I made my way between the two. I was pumped up and ready for anything.

Which is why it came as a bit of a shock when, an hour and a half later, I was stood on the dock at Calais feeling about as lonely as I had ever felt in my life. Jim the Scottish salmon man had taken a left to Luxembourg – somewhere I had decided that I didn't want to go – and I was once again on my own.

Being on my own was nothing unusual, after all, that was the way it had been since I left Manchester 17 hours previously. In France, though, something felt different. Instead of feeling like The Man, I most definitely felt like The Boy. The Cold Boy, too: with no jacket I was forced to do a Michelin Man impression and put all my clothes on at once.

My mental state was equally unprepared. The loneliness hooked into my mind, refusing to be shaken off with the little pep-talks I was giving myself. My mind was playing ping-pong with itself, and the Dark Destroyer of Doubt seemed to be giving Blind Hope a right royal whipping.

'You'll be fine,' the line went.

'You know nobody in this country,' came the reply.

'You've got away from Manchester and now the world is for yer taking.'

'You're an easy target.'

'Cheer up. It might never happen.'

'You'll probably wind up dead.'

Game over. Not a good start to my European Tour.

All this was going on while I was trying to hitch myself a lift. I didn't know where I wanted to go – I wasn't fussy – but it still took me three hours to get off the tarmac and into a warm cab. It was about 5.30 a.m. and I'd been without sleep for far too long. Needless to say, I wasn't in the mood for talking.

I woke up in Paris. That's not strictly true – my first lift took me to some industrial town a few miles north of Paris. Rolling out of the cab, I stood at a junction and waited for something else to come along. I stumbled into the next truck that stopped. I'm not sure how long I waited, but I think I managed to do it all without waking up too much.

Paris seemed like as good a place as any to start, so I spent a few days there. Not that I was taking in the galleries or writing bad poetry in a café; my days were far more basic. I'd sleep in a park at night, covering myself with newspapers, boxes or whatever else I could find to try and keep warm. In the day I'd hide my rucksack and go about my business of acquiring food.

That meant thieving, and while I'd been known to dabble in the art of the quick fingers back home (usually in my mum's purse or behind the back of some moody shopkeeper), the stakes had never been quite as high. I knew that getting caught would probably see me sent back to England, but I also knew that if I didn't steal I'd be starting to get ill. If man's basic needs are food, warmth and shelter, I figured that while I was failing miserably with two of them, I owed it to myself to keep up the payments with the other.

With the rucksack hidden away somewhere, I was ready – if necessary – to do a runner without all that extra weight. It also meant that I didn't look quite so much like a desperate kid who'd run away from Manchester and spent all his money in motorway service stations and on fruit machines. My thieving plan was simple: firstly, I was only gonna take what I absolutely needed. Secondly, I would only nick stuff that wasn't difficult to carry. Have you ever tried concealing a French stick up yer jumper? It was hard to be inconspicuous, and even harder to make a getaway without leaving a tell-tale trail of crumbs behind me.

After a few close shaves – mad Frenchmen shouting and chasing me down the street, me feeling like something out of a

Benny Hill sketch – I decided to revise part two of my plan. I moved on to items that could be concealed a little better than a three-foot loaf, and for a couple of days I lived on nothing but chewing gum and pâté.

I was desperate though. I reckon if I had got caught I would have fought like a wild beast, I was that hungry. Anyway, Paris wasn't really doing it for me and I couldn't see what all the fuss was about. I decided to leave, and found myself in Lyons. That wasn't much cop either. OK, so it felt a little bit further away from home than Dover, Calais or Paris, but at first sight it just didn't seem to have what I was looking for. Not that I knew what I was looking for, but it just didn't have it.

There was another reason why I wasn't that into Lyons. The hitching was starting to get to me and I was generally feeling pretty nervous and uneasy about things. Getting into a cab with a total stranger and sitting in silence for a couple of hours was not exactly my idea of fun. I used to wonder what they were thinking, whether they were planning on jumping me or whether they were worrying about me jumping them. I hadn't washed for days and I absolutely reeked. I think it's fair to say that they were probably more worried about me, and I'm sure a few of them regretted pulling over in the first place.

Because of this, I had mixed feelings about my next destination. What I wanted was a bit of heat, so I decided to head for Spain. If I hesitated and started thinking about how much I hated hitching, I might never have left, but I was desperate. I had no choice but to hitch it – evading fares on the railway was too risky and nicking a car was just too stupid. I wanted to get to Spain, where I pictured myself sunbathing by palm trees, being waited on by dark-haired maidens. I'd seemed to have forgotten that it was February, but the dream was enough to get me moving.

I'd never been one for geography while I was at school, and this next leg of the journey brought me face to face with some serious regrets about my behaviour in Miss Johnstone's class. It had never occurred to me that travelling to Spain might mean passing through the mountainous region covered by Andorra. While it might have been great for skiing, it was not so pleasant for a young lad from Manchester with only two jumpers to his name. Believe me, minus 10 was not good.

My lift had dropped me off within a few miles of the French border with Andorra, and in a desperate attempt to keep the cold out, I'd wrapped one jumper around my head. I probably didn't look at my best. To put it mildly, I was surprised when a little MG sports car pulled up and the driver told me to get in. He couldn't have been more than a few years older than me and he seemed sound enough. I got in, and within minutes I was in heaven. The tunes were blaring out, and he pulled out a joint loaded with some cheeky weed. The car was full of smoke, and just as I'd started to relax, he must have flicked his Stirling Moss switch, 'cos we were flying round these snake passes, many covered with ice and snow. He was flinging the car from side to side, taking corners about as tight as he could and hammering the gears like a regular psychopath. I told him that I thought he ought to slow down.

'But I love the sensation of fear, no?' he said in a stoned, Swiss kind of way.

I grabbed my seatbelt to put it on, but as I went to click it in, he grabbed my hand and gave me the wildest of looks.

'Don't you trust me?' he asked.

I mumbled something back, but in my mind the answer was clear: NO WAY, PSYCHO BOY. I muttered something about just wanting to get across Andorra in one piece, but for the rest of the journey he refused to let me buckle up. Suddenly minus 10 with a jumper round my head didn't seem like such a bad way to cross the mountains after all. He ignored my pleas to be let out, and after a while I went back to smoking with my eyes shut.

We pulled up to the border and I stayed in the car while my driver was asked to get out by the guards. I sat there wondering how far I'd have to stay with him before we reached another place where I could start hitching again. The border guards checked the boot and all that, and after a while we were allowed to drive on through into Spain. This bloke was laughing to himself as we crossed, and once we were in he told me to take a look under my seat. I wondered why, and it slowly dawned on me what was going on.

What I found confused me though. There was a black bag full of walkie-talkies. Matey boy was laughing manically by now, and I took the first opportunity I could to get out and hurl a few insults at him as he sped away. It was only a few months later – when I'd become a little better acquainted with the ways of drug dealers in the area – that I knew what was going on. The walkie-talkies were central to any decent drugs outfit in the Pyrenees. Smugglers and dealers relied on them to be able to communicate, and the police had just cottoned on. Unregistered walkie-talkies – broadcasting on illegal bands – were therefore bad news, as was smuggling them in. I, of course, was the perfect dummy. If they'd been found then the driver would have easily been able to pass the blame on to me – the rough-looking hitch-hiker obviously desperate for money – and walk away scot free. I, on the other hand, would have had to fight against the evidence that I was involved in some major drug distribution.

This was, as they say, a low. It just seemed that there were too many risks, too many chances that I could wind up in trouble with the law or worse. So that last guy was some kind of nutter, but what next? Would I be taking lifts from mass murderers? Would I end up the unfortunate star of some driller-killer movie? I seriously questioned whether it was worth all the hassle. Tough as it would be, maybe I was better off going back home and facing the consequences.

For about four hours I sat by the road, not bothering to try and get a lift, just chewing over the situation and feeling hungry. The comedown from the spliff had left me with some serious munchies, and as if I was in any doubt before, my stomach was now going ballistic with wanting something inside it.

But for all the whingeing my stomach was doing, my mind was concentrating on other things. They say that travel broadens it. For me, this first bit of journeying away from home with no option to return just about destroyed it. I'd always been a bit of an optimist, always believing that the great plans inside my head would one day come about. This was the first time that the gap between dreaming something and living it out had been so short, and it did me in to realize that not everything in life matched up to my high expectations. I don't know how I thought it was gonna happen, but I'd been convinced that running away from Wythenshawe was gonna be some kind of easy-life adventure. I tell you, by the time I got out of the MG inside Spain, I was feeling like the most god-forsaken loser around.

It was the basic need for warmth that kept me going. As far as I could tell, I was cold, tired and hungry. I had no money and I didn't feel safe sleeping on the hard shoulder, so I decided to do what I could and sort at least one of my problems out. Back home was warm, but it meant going through Andorra again, and nothing was gonna get me back in that minus-10 hellhole. So I headed south.

I hitched a while. The first place I ended up in worth mentioning was Salou, a coastal town that had a little too much in common with Skegness for my liking. I don't know what I was thinking, but I remember feeling let down that my first Spanish resort town wasn't all turquoise sea, white sand and beautiful locals moving seductively between palm trees. Instead it was all John Bull pubs and all-day breakfasts, OAPs from Bridlington and boarded-up shops.

Still, this was probably a good thing, as I soon found out that like any half-decent resort town, there were a handful of clubs desperate to do something to get the punters in. I visited them all and made them my offer: a three-minute breakdancing demonstration for a few quid and a hot shower. I got five no's, three slammed doors and one yes. It suited me fine and I got £15 for my first night's work.

My plan was to pocket the money and be on my way the next morning, off to find somewhere better. I didn't know what it was that I wanted, but I knew Salou didn't have it. If the journey so far was gonna be worth it, I'd have to end up in somewhere pretty special, somewhere at least that had a bit of life.

The people in the club must have known that I had nowhere to stay that night, but I was too proud to ask for help. They didn't bring it up either, and by the state of me I can't say that I blamed them. I don't know what they must have thought, but I was happier kipping under a bridge than taking a chance with more strangers. After I'd done my turn on the mat I pocketed the cash and left.

I was green when I was younger, but this trip was helping to sort me out. I can remember wagging school one day with my mate Dominic, and we were sitting on some statue, I think it was Queen Victoria's in the centre of Manchester. A man approached us, looking like he'd just stepped off the set of *The Good Life*. I was about to congratulate him on his fine choice of three-tone brown jumper when he stopped and cleared his throat.

'Arright lads?'

'Arright there, Mr BHS,' I replied, hoping that Dominic would find the line half as funny as I did.

Brown-man was not deterred. 'How do you two fancy earning some money? I've got some boxes that need moving just round

59

the corner and I'll give you a couple of quid each if you lend us a hand.'

I was well up for it, and I was just about to jump up and follow when Dominic started shouting at him.

The bloke went pale as a ghost and ran off. It took a while for Dominic to explain that he was probably some kind of paedophile after some young lads. It taught me a lesson, but in the years that followed I was continually having to stop myself from running away with my gullible instincts.

I'm here trying to sleep. That unofficial day's holiday from school is playing in my mind. I can remember it all; the laughter as the bloke ran off and the fear as Dominic explained what might have happened. I haven't got a clue. I'm cold. I'm tired and I haven't got a clue. What the hell am I doing here? Why have I done this? What's going to happen to me? If I keep trusting strangers I could end up dead. But I can't make it on my own. I can't make it on my own.

But the images of that day off give way to memories of what I've left behind: a whole heap of trouble and someone waiting to pull my limbs off should I dare show my face again. Trapped? You could say that. Colonel Abrahams, you know the score. And you know what? I do feel like a fool; if I'd had a bit more sense about me I wouldn't be cold and hungry like this right now. This is one educational experience they didn't prepare me for at school.

COKE

Barcelona was about as different from Salou as you could get. Don't know why it surprised me so much at the time, but I remember standing in the city open-mouthed. I'd been given a lift by a couple of students and was dropped off at the main station. It was all there for me to see: prostitutes, businessmen and dark-haired blokes standing around looking hard – a regular railway station cliché.

Now, I was a pretty young lad in those days – pretty enough to get my fair share of weirdos offering me anything from sex where they paid me to sex where I paid them. I wanted none of it, and by the time I'd got over the surprise of being in a buzzing city again – even though I'd been in Paris just a few days before – I realized I was back to square one: hungry.

So far on this continental journey I must admit that my thieving wasn't up to much. My performance in Paris had been well below the standards I'd reached in my youth. Back in Wythenshawe I was working towards calling myself a top blagger, nicking anything from Armani suits and jeans to – well, it was pretty much Armani suits and jeans really. Anyway, me and everyone else I knew were of a similar frame of mind: if you were gonna get caught, it was worth getting caught for something big. Imagine the shame of being collared by the Old Bill for a couple of Mars bars and a bottle of Tippex.

In Barcelona something changed. I sussed out that I might be able to do more than just keep my belly half-full with the thieving. With a selection of sleepy-looking shop owners to keep me stocked up and a whole load of tourists on the streets who looked like they'd buy everything, I was sure I could rob from the not so rich and sell to the not so poor. A regular supply-and-demand Robin Hood.

My technique was simple: if it was small, expensive and not bolted down, I'd nick it. That meant I suddenly developed a keen interest in photography. Unfortunately, having only had one shower in almost 10 days I didn't look like much of a David Bailey. I was forced to use the 'grab and run' technique. Shame, as I'd always thought the best results came from working as part of a team – you know the score, one lad asking the shopkeeper to fetch various items from the shelves behind, with the partner loading his pockets as soon as Mr Shopkeeper's back was turned. But teamwork was not on the menu. So instead I'd walk in, check out for security cameras, browse for a while, make my selection and leg it. Then it would be off to find some English tourists. Maybe it was all that sun, sangria and fast-disappearing holiday money that made them do it, but each time I approached them with the offer of a £150 camera, in its box, for a tenner, John Bull just smiled and reached for his wallet.

I was glad too; much as I knew I was probably closer to being 'one of them' than I'd have liked to admit, I didn't really fancy doing any business transactions with the local Barcelona street people. Nah, Johnny Foreigner would suit me just fine: no questions, no style and no problem.

With the ill-gotten gains of four transactions lining my pockets, I left Barcelona with a single destination in mind:

Coke

Alicante. All right, so it might have been as tacky then as it is now, all Brits abroad and sunburnt arses, but for a young lad from Manchester, it was my kind of town. It was probably something to do with the fact that it was the only Spanish city I'd heard of, but even as I arrived I knew I could do something there. The city had none of the cosmopolitan chic of Barcelona, nor could it compete with the sheer size of Paris. Instead it was the kind of place that ran on the McDonald's principle: don't give the punters too much to choose from and keep everything cheap. As I walked around what I thought must have been the main square, all I could see were tacky discos, English pubs and cafés serving food just like mum made back home.

Home. It got me thinking, and for the first time I started to feel a bit sad. Until then I'd been either on the run, starving, seriously fed up or too stoned to care. Now things were getting a bit clearer and I wondered what my family would be thinking. They knew I was off on my travels, but were they worrying? Of course, everyone likes to have a bit of worrying done about them from time to time, and I was no different. A few sleepless nights and teary-eyed looks at my photo on the wall ought to do it. But things don't change that easily, or at least they don't for me. I was still there, still lonely, still missing friends and family back home. But more than the people, I missed the feelings that went with it: I missed feeling safe.

It didn't take me long to snap out of it and return to matters in hand. I was hungry (no surprise there), skint (again, not exactly a surprise) and not looking forward to the prospect of another night sleeping on a beach (the usual). It was mid-morning by the time I arrived and the first thing I did was to find somewhere safe to store my rucksack. An overgrown bush on the edge of a park did the trick and I made my way back towards the clubs I'd seen earlier.

In my mind I had a little plan: get a bit of work breakdancing in clubs, top up the cash with some stealing from shops just outside Alicante. I wasn't that happy about the stealing bit, but I knew I didn't have much choice.

First stop when I'd got into town was a bar. It was empty apart from the usual owner gently polishing the bar with a tea towel draped over his shoulder – not quite *Casablanca*, but good enough. He looked sound enough so I gave him the speech.

"Ere mate, can you 'elp us out? I've had a bit of a 'ard time.'

He looked at me for a while and told me he could see that I'd had it a bit rough. Instead of laughing about it he said something unexpected. He told me that before anything else he'd get me sorted out with a decent meal.

'Chips all right?'

'All right? Feast for kings, mate.' I was blown away. By his accent I could tell he was a regular southern lad – probably Southampton or somewhere like that – and what he was doing out there I'll never know. Strange, but it surprised me to find someone else out there who wasn't just a tourist. For some reason I thought I was the only English bloke who'd ever had the idea of popping down to Spain to kill the double bird: get away from life back home and fill up the pockets with some easy cash. I wasn't sure what he'd left behind, – and I didn't much care – he seemed to be doing all right on the cash front and I was more than happy to test his hospitality.

Of course, it wouldn't take long before I realized just how wrong my expectations had been about meeting other Brits in Spain. Without them I reckon the whole economy could have gone under – or the shadier aspects of it at least. Over the years I saw more Brits making more money out of Spain than I'd ever thought possible, most of it to do with drugs. It was a regular crusade, only this time it wasn't horses and swords, but mopeds and charlie.

But I'm jumping ahead of myself a bit here. After he'd fed me we had a chat. I was busy trying to tell him all about my breakdancing plan, but he had other ideas about my next move. He told me about a mate who had a flat for rent. It was cheap for Alicante – so he told me – and the rent of 10 mil worked out at about £50 per week. It sounded a bit much to me, but what did I know about the renting market in southern Spain? He told me that he'd put a word in and get me the place without having to pay any rent up front, leaving me a week to raise the 10 mil. I wondered whether he was trying to do me over, but here I was, back in that old familiar corner: trust no one and end up who knows where or take a risk and end up – well, that was exactly the problem. I could picture one outcome: he knew I couldn't raise the cash so he'd bail me out at the end of the week and have me doing whatever he wanted until I'd paid him off. My mind filled in a few blanks as to what that 'whatever he wanted' might be. I winced every time, but it was still worth the risk. At the end of the day, I told myself, I could always do a bunk before the end of the week. Of course, I knew I was running out of towns, but I tried not to think on it too much.

Sod it, I thought, and we did the deal. He took me to the flat and I took a step back in amazement. It wasn't just that it had a roof and all that, but it had a shower, a kind of kitchen and all the things that a young lad could want: a bed, a table for skinning up on and a few rolls of bog paper. I was beginning to think this guy might be all right, and in the following weeks that I knew him I never changed my mind. He'd seen it all before: young lads running from something without a clue of how to survive. I never found out if it was something he'd been through himself, but maybe he was just a nice guy through and through.

I spent a day doing nothing much: having showers, sleeping and getting my clothes washed. The bloke had lent me about a mil, which was just enough to sort me out for the week. I didn't want to push it with him, and as he'd already heard my break-dancing pitch but had failed to offer me any work, I decided to find some for myself. I managed to get about five gigs that week, just by asking club and bar owners if they were up for it. Some I played up the hard luck angle, but others I hit them with it straight: I was a genius breakdancer who just happened to be in town in between international engagements. If they were lucky I might just be able to give them a quick demonstration, but only as a favour. Oh, and by the way, if they could spare 15 quid as payment that would go down just fine. I think I actually believed that they were taken in by it, which is embarrassing enough in itself.

For the first couple of shows I got pretty excited walking up to the venue to see my name in chalk on the board outside. Obviously no one spelt it correctly – Comeon Dancing was my favourite – but I still managed to get a little rush in my ego. Things brought me down to earth when I started to do the gigs, as let's face it, it wasn't quite New York. The family audience would be sat on their white plastic garden furniture, singing along to the latest Dire Straits, Sinitta or Stock, Aitken and Waterman hit. I'd get a quick intro and then I'd be on. I had five minutes in which to impress, accompanied by some seriously unimpressive tunes limping out of the speaker. It was a long way from the pulsating, charged atmosphere of the old competitions. Here it was more shellsuit than tracksuit, and if I was lucky I got a polite round of applause after I'd sweated my guts out with Headspins, Windmills and a couple of crack Thomson Flares.

The first week went OK, and I got enough cash in to pay the rent and pay back my benefactor. Things got better over the next couple of weeks as some kind of demand seemed to grow for my routines. This came as a surprise, but a pretty welcome one. I was doing two a night, earning a bit of cash and finally managing to get on top of things.

I'd be lying if I said that I saw it coming. I was too busy enjoying the buzz to work anything else out, and by the end of that three-week period I was back where I started. I'd become yesterday's news and suddenly there were no more gigs. This was not to be the first time that I experienced the fickle nature of the buzz: one moment it's on you like a rash and everyone's into yer stuff. The next you might as well be stuffing live hand-grenades up yer arse for all the attention it'll get you, and people just don't want to know. Back in Alicante this started a simple chain reaction: with no more gigs there was no more money and that meant kissing goodbye to my apartment. It had been fun while it had lasted, but there was no time to get sentimental: I was back on the streets and needed a solution fast.

Once I'd stopped staring at my name on the blackboard, I'd noticed a strange bunch of people hanging around the clubs. They were a right pick 'n' mix; junkies and alkies to people who'd held down good jobs once upon a time but saw the need to get out of the rat race. They were known as propaganda. It was up to them to get people off the streets and into the clubs, and for their trouble they'd get no better than a mil (about a fiver) each night. It was tough work – not for the shy and retiring – and it was pretty much the bottom rung of the ladder.

Earning a mil a night for seven days of the week meant that the propaganda boys couldn't even afford to rent their own rooms, so you'd get loads of them chipping in and renting an apartment between them. With ten blokes in a two-roomed apartment there wasn't much in the way of privacy, and it was pretty normal for their gear to get nicked, their 'beds' to get taken over or their sleep to get totally ruined by some randy couple just a few feet away. It was rough, and after the break-dancing work dried up, it was about my only hope.

I managed to get work without too much trouble, and signed up for a life of no privacy by moving into one of the propaganda flats. I'd come home having worked from five in the afternoon through to four in the morning to find my bed full of flour, tooth-paste and whatever else my comedy flatmates could think of using. I don't remember laughing much.

I was probably one of the better guys in the team: I was younger, a bit more desperate and less bothered about making a total fool of myself in public. I did too, and soon had my own technique sorted for getting people in. It involved flirting and not much more. OK, so it wasn't much of a technique, but it seemed to work all right for me.

Life in the apartment didn't take long to get me down. They were a nightmare to live with and I was fed up of all of it. Everything was just that little bit too much of an all-lads-together cliché.

'Who's nicked my shorts?' I'd ask from time to time.

'Me,' would come the reply from Deano, Mally, Dimmo or Stiffy. 'I used them when we ran out of bog roll.' And they wouldn't be joking.

In fact, the whole thing revolved around the toilet: covering the bowl with cling-film, hiding records down there while I'd been out, leaving used condoms as evidence of their marathon stag-like love-feats all over the floor. It was too much. I mean, I liked the guys, but just not that much.

I took my chance and told the manager that unless he found me somewhere else to live I'd be off. I scored half a result as he said he'd get me into another, better apartment, but not for a week or two. In the meantime he told me I could sleep in the basement. There were a couple of camp beds down there, and I was sharing it with Andreas, one of the Spanish barmen. There was no ventilation, it was red hot and full of mosquitoes which, when they weren't lit by the single bare lightbulb hanging from the ceiling, could be felt taking a quick toke on yer arm or leg. By the end of the week I was in a worse state than when I'd arrived in Alicante.

68

Coke

Things got better by the end of the week though, and the manager let me move into a new apartment. How could I afford it? That was the best bit of luck I'd had all trip as a few things seemed to be helping my cause. First up was the manager himself: he happened to notice me giving it the 'arright darlin'?' on the street and he was apparently impressed. Then there was the resident DJ: he'd just been done for working without a permit and had been sent back to Stoke with his record bag between his legs. And there was the current flavour of the month: gobby DJs who could play a few crowd-pleasing tunes and get the drinkers hyped up.

My lucky day was the Friday. I'd been off all day, trying to get as far away from Andreas as possible, when I turned up back at the club to be pulled over to one side by the boss. He took me to one end of the bar, played with his cufflinks and gave it to me straight.

'You know you make a good DJ.'

'Oh yeah. Yeah. Definitely. No problem.' I was lying my arse off and desperately hoped that he wouldn't notice.

'You've never done it but I know you make good DJ, yes?'

'Um. No, mate. I'm a top deejay.' More lying.

'So I give you 10 thousand pesetas every night and you be new DJ, yes?'

He didn't have to wait long for my answer; just the thought of getting away from working on the street was enough to make me go for it. The money? Well, let's just say it was an additional incentive.

Now I need to be straight about this right from the start. I don't want you thinking this was some kind of Pascha or Manumission: this was Club 18-30 in all its pink-fleshed glory, or is that gory? This was 1988 and Ibiza was just taking off. Dance music was doing its thing, but pop was still the main tune being played from this club's PA. It was lager, sex, Madonna and

Whitney. It was games on the stage and fights at the end of the night. It was a dance floor sticky with beer and in those early days, the blokes had to be totally bladdered to dance. There was no style, no class. But it suited me at the time.

I nearly came unstuck before I started though. The boss asked me to get up into the booth straight away and do him a couple of mixes. Even though he knew I was blagging it when I told him I was plenty experienced I reckon he just wanted a laugh at my expense. I wasn't a total novice; I did have some kind of idea how it worked, and I'd probably had a few goes while killing time at breakdancing competitions, but I was no Pete Tong. Getting up into the booth that night I wouldn't say that I mixed the tracks, more like I slammed another one down on the deck as soon as I thought we were running out of time with the first one. Tempo and rhythm? Forget it, mate. But I was well away with the mic, shouting out something incomprehensible. It made the boss laugh and after half an hour of getting the crowd to do the Lambada I was led back to the bar and given a few drinks. I was buzzing. It was my kind of deal and I knew I'd found something I was good at. That felt pretty good, I can tell you.

Come to think of it, I don't think I can have passed the test with flying colours. We agreed that I'd make my debut on Sunday, but when the big night came around I was told that I wouldn't need to bother touching the records. Instead I was on the mic all night long giving it all the gob that I could manage. I'd done a bit of MCing before and I could rap if I had to. Actually I only had one rap, but I wasn't afraid to use and reuse it. It was a simple number, totally clichéd and nicked from Rhino: *Cam-er-on is my name I'm the king of rap lyrics flow from my mouth like water out of a tap.*

I was soon into it and had got the hang of making a half-decent attempt at convincing people that I knew my way around the turntables. I also got more and more brave on the mic. Each night there was a Crazy Hour – 12 till 1. The idea was simple: get people even more bladdered and get as many girls as possible up on stage with their tops off. It was a neat little marketing strategy, as a clear view of a stage full of topless birds was bound to attract plenty of roaming lads. The roaming lads spent all their money at the bar and everyone was happy. Here's how the hour kicked off:

Track one: conga. Get everyone up and about and flirting with each other, gentle crotch-rubbing and all that.

Track two: Simple Minds. Get the lads shouting and jumping up and down in groups. Get the girls bouncing.

Track three: 'Oops Upside Yer Head'. Get them doing the actions and building up a thirst. More groping.

While they were still sitting down I'd shout out that the first girl to stand up and whip her top off wins a bottle of champagne. Ten of them would do it and you were under way. One thing would lead to another and bingo – live sex, and we didn't even have to pay. Manumission may get the attention for it now, but there were plenty of places like The Bahamas at it long before.

Of course this was illegal and if we got caught the club could have been shut down. But the manager must have thought it was a risk worth taking as each night there were queues outside of people waiting to get in. In Alicante that was unusual: I mean, clubs weren't exactly hard to find. But The Bahamas was doing something different and the people loved it. As I said, not quite Pete Tong, but you've got to start somewhere, right?

The boss was loving it, although our arrival in the world of live sex and rocketing bar receipts attracted the attention of the local police. Of course he had to start paying them off, but the price of their silence was a lot less than the amount of cash that was crossing over the bar each night. I wasn't really sure how much he was paying them, but the figure £1,500 a night seems to be in my mind. I don't know: that sounds like a lot of money to me, but then again, The Bahamas was a big club, well capable of having a couple of thousand punters in there. With the place rammed every night with people getting seriously bladdered, maybe it wasn't such a lot of money after all.

All this time I was learning how to mix, finding out that there was more to it than slapping a few tunes down onto the turntable. After a month of seven nights a week playing from 7 at night till 7 a.m., I worked out that I needed some kind of safety net. All the propaganda boys were wizzing their heads off, and they used to sort me out too. It doesn't take a genius to work out that me, wizz and a microphone was bound to be an interesting combination. My output doubled as I refused to shut up. I was screaming down the mic, getting people even more hyped up than before. I was no longer just a big-gob foghorn: I was a big-gob foghorn who kept going all night.

One evening before I started the boss called me into his office. It was a broom cupboard and nothing more, just about big enough to house his desk, which didn't look like it was the venue for that much work. After a while he spoke up:

'You're good now. You talk good.'

'Yeah, thanks,' I said. I realized that I didn't actually know his name. I felt uncomfortable. I knew what he was saying and I was bricking it. I knew nothing about him – certainly a lot less than I'd find out later – and I didn't know how he'd react to having a DJ off his face on wizz all night every night. I didn't exactly think of him as being a saint, but you never knew what sort of pet hates people had.

I couldn't have been more wrong about José Carlos. He walked to a filing cabinet, unlocked it and brought out a bag – almost as big as a regular carrier bag – which he put on the desk in front of me. I assumed that the white powder inside was wizz, my new best friend, so I was naturally pleased when he scooped out a line that ran the length of the desk.

Coke

'This is the best you find in Alicante,' he told me. 'No question about it: the best in Alicante.' He chuckled to himself as he made the final preparations to the line, saying 'best in Alicante' as if he'd only just learnt how to laugh.

When it was ready he stopped and looked me in the eye. 'With this you work even better. Even more talk, OK?'

I think I understood what he was going on about. I didn't like to tell him that I was already wizzing it when I was on the mic and a nagging thought settled itself down in the back of my mind: if he was expecting to see some kind of difference now that I'd had some of his wizz, he might just be disappointed. I decided that there was only one way around it: take on board as much of the stuff as I possibly could.

Instead of the usual wizz taste in the back of my mouth, the one which never failed to get me hissing like a snake as I tried to get rid of it, this time my nose and throat went numb. It made a change, but not a very nice one. I thought I was dying, that I'd somehow snorted a hole right through my neck and was about to collapse.

'Hey,' said José Carlos. 'You like cocaine? Is good, uh? Best in Alicante.' In between chuckles he finished off what I'd left.

I was in a panic, fretting about what I'd just done as well as about the fact that not only was I clearly on the verge of death, but I was due up in the booth to get things started. I was not in a good state when I left that office. Certain that this was about to be the biggest DJing disaster ever, I prepared myself for the fact that this would be my farewell gig. But by the time I'd got into my little home from home, I was on fire. For twelve hours I was a ranting, swearing, jumping, dancing, screaming, surfing, strutting, staring, spinning, grinning, scowling, smoking, drinking MASTER. I was up, up and away and I was THE MAN. Nothing was bringing me down, and with the few grams I had transferred from José Carlos's desktop to my fizzling system, I didn't even need the wrap of charlie he placed in my hand halfway through. I put it straight in the pocket and carried on doing my thing. It was pure madness and I was mad for it.

By the time I got home I noticed something different: whereas I'd usually need a quick line of wizz when I got home to keep me from feeling as rough as Gandhi's slippers, on coke I was ready for a kip. This was a welcome relief, and I woke up the next day feeling better than I did on wizz. In fact, I reached into my pocket and pulled out the unused wrap from the night before.

I'd never taken coke before, not because I thought it was worse than wizz or whatever, but simply because of the price. I'd never been able to afford it, but after these first couple of times I knew that was no excuse: somehow I'd have to move up the drug-consuming ladder and sort myself out with this more expensive habit. Not only was the high so much higher than with wizz, but the comedown was nowhere near as bad. There was no diar-rhoea, no stomach cramps and I'd been able to sleep (almost) as soon as I'd wanted to.

After an afternoon being tickled by the wrap, I went into work. Before I had the chance to find him he found me and invited me into his office. This time there was no sack of coke on the desk or communal session, but he did give me a nod, a wink and a small plastic bag with what looked like three or four grams in it. As charlie was going for about £80 per gram round there, let's just say I knew on what side my bread was buttered.

Things kept on going like this for a good couple of months, and all the time the buzz just seemed to get bigger and bigger. Not only was I finally managing to mix the records without it sounding like a herd of buffalo, I was also getting on better with all the propaganda lads. We'd go out during the day – dosing up on tequila slammers – and what with the difference in our two incomes (like me having one and them not), it wasn't long before my days became one long hardcore party ship with me hanging from the rigging unable to do anything but enjoy the view and soak up the fun.

Now of course, it won't take a genius to work out that the summer of '88 took a leading role in the history of club culture. It was all kicking off nicely in Ibiza and Club Shoom back in London, but Alicante? Let's just say the mainland Spanish had managed to put their own unique twist to things. In the pursuit of having a mad one, me and my propaganda mates were always on the hunt to check out what few clubs would be open when we'd all finished up at The Bahamas. One day we struck gold in the form of a dingy, seedy-looking locals' club called Black Sabbad. These locals' clubs were pretty much off limits for tourists and were full instead of the local Spaniards. And us.

We turned up and were well into it from the moment we walked down the stairs. It was playing Bachalau – a type of music that had been big in the Spanish underground dance culture for a while. It was classed as top-notch drug music by the locals and the DJ would weave his magic spells by hooking up a drum machine and playing bits of The Cure and Front 242 over the top. It was mad, and it certainly made a nice change from 'Itsy Bitsy Teeny Weeny Yellow Polka-Dot Bikini'.

Now those propaganda lads never had much money, so coke was out of the question for a visit to Black Sabbad, and as they'd been wizzing their faces off all night trying to get people into The Bahamas, they naturally wanted something a little different. It so happened that trips were dirt cheap round there, so as soon as the end of work approached and a Black Sabbad session loomed, they'd start necking the acid in preparation.

It paid off once they were in the club, too: the tunes and the dark, seedy venue made for a tasty atmosphere, especially when it was full of Spaniards and prop lads doing the Bachalau dance. Later on you'd see the same thing at any E-fuelled club as people stood, rooted to the spot, moving their heads from side to side, arms half-outstretched, mouths like an O and eyes all surprised. Bachalau was just the same but without the eyes and mouth. People would stare at the floor, shaking their heads from side to side to the 4/4 beat. Simple as that. Add a few trips to the mix and you've got yourself a 100 per cent intense head job.

For some reason I didn't join in with the trips – I never have been much of a one for all that manic giggling and sanity-dissolving chatter. I've always preferred things more physical, more UP, so after a night of charlie at The Bahamas I'd dose myself up a bit more and let it all go at Black Sabbad. I'd also started DJing there, so trips were definitely off the menu. I might have been having a laugh, screaming and shouting and grinning like a prize gurner, but I knew there were limits when I was on the job. Acid was mine.

I wish I could say that it was my skills on the old wheels of steel that had got me the gig, but the truth is that it was more about supply and demand. It turned out that the coked-up locals had been keeping Black Sabbad ticking over for years, shaking their heads to the Bachalau beat and all that. Once tripping John Bull turned up in the form of us propaganda lads, the head-shaking carried on but the hands were in the air and the shouts of delight and excitement certainly turned up the heat. Suddenly the seedy side was overtaken by an atmosphere of hardcore drug-induced fever. It hadn't taken long for word to spread, and early on as many as fifty of us would turn up at 7 a.m. Money would be spent and, as I said, the whole vibe of the place took on a British feel. But the manager noticed that the Brits liked their music a certain way: plenty of 303 acid blips to make their trip just that little bit more special. Enter me, stage left, and as the only English DJ around consuming enough drugs to be up for a new session as the sun rose, the job was mine.

Now you might be wondering just how well the Spanish and Brits got on. To tell you the truth it was beautiful. We weren't like the rest of the lagered-up giddies – the name the locals gave the easily excited British tourists – and they could see that we were just there for a mad one, keen to have a laugh. We all got on well, and apart from the odd misunderstanding about women or drugs, things went pretty smoothly throughout. After all, we were lining the manager's pockets and keeping the rest of the clubbers amused, so why spoil it?

When things started out for me at Black Sabbad I'd just take to the decks for an hour or two, chucking out whatever tunes from back home I had on me. As things got better and better I got to play for longer and I started to put more effort into getting the latest releases. Alicante was a write-off as far as record purchases were concerned, so I found myself getting in touch with Spinnin' Records back home, and chucking them 50 or 100 quid a month to send us over a box of the greatest and latest. I wanted them big, and the boy came up trumps every time. We had 'Acid Thunder' by Fast Eddie, 'Acid Over' by Tyree as well as Kraze's 'The Party'. I'll never forget the spine-tingling excitement of putting 'Chime' by Orbital on the turntable for the first time. It was strange never having heard these tunes in the flesh before, and there was something odd about putting them on for the first time in my apartment alone of an afternoon. I reckon it was a good way of sussing things out though, and if a record got me going in that clinical environment I knew it was a winner.

You've probably worked out that I was happy at Black Sabbad. I wasn't getting paid but at least it was the chance to do what I really wanted to do, playing the tunes that I liked rather than be Mr Cabaret Man back at The Bahamas. That meant I was up for doing as much as I could at Black Sabbad, and towards the end of the season I was playing throughout the morning and into the afternoon. Helping me down from the charlie were free shots of whisky courtesy of the manager, and so by the time I finished I was a total wreck.

But it felt worth it at the time. I was a bit torn though; The Bahamas was bringing in some decent cash – so much that I'd even risked it with the law by opening a bank account. I was on £350 a week for part of the season, rising to £700 later on. I was paying nothing for my drugs and spending £50 on rent and probably a fraction of that on food. The rest of my life was one big blag and now we were all spending our days at Black Sabbad I hardly even had to put my hand in my pocket. By the end of the season I must have saved up three or four grand – a tasty sum at any time – and it made the amount of work I was doing bearable. To be honest, I knew that if push came to shove – while I was loving the fantasy of being a proper club DJ – Black Sabbad would have to take a back seat to The Bahamas. That was my cash cow and she needed plenty of milking.

This is where things started to go a bit wrong. I found out that in making charlie my new best friend, there were one or two side effects that came with it. It was a top social buzz and all that, and like my old boss at The Bahamas, I developed the Wrigley's approach: great to snort, better to share. I'd be forever dishing out the lines, giving the wink and nose-point to a mate, sorting them out with a gram and a handshake. Of course, the Pied Piper's always the most popular guy in town, and I started hanging out with lots of the locals. Pretty soon I'd met some of the big boys on the shadier side of Alicante life: the gun-carrying doormen who'd all served stretches for murder; the smacked-up club owners who would stop at nothing in their pursuit of cash; the drug baron whose pet iguana had a diamond-studded collar. OK, I made that last bit up, but you get the picture.

I'd known my fair share of villains back home, and it was precisely because I knew them that I'd done a bunk and wound up here. I didn't fancy getting involved in the criminal underworld again – I told myself that as I sweated in my apartment – but somehow I just couldn't stay away. Perhaps the coke was to blame, or perhaps it was my character. Maybe fate played a part, or then again it might just have been a fluke. Either way, as that first season came to a close my life was very different from the start.

I bought myself a motorbike, and like the bank account, I knew this was illegal – I had no licence (fake or legit) – and it was just another excuse for the police to use to kick me out of the country. But they didn't touch me. There I was, bombing about the town like a pillock and no one said a word. I'd be off my face, falling off as yet another attempt at a wheely to impress the ladies ended in failure, and the bizzies turned a blind eye. I was confused, of course, but at first it never occurred to me to wonder why. Thinking about it now it all makes sense: the manager was paying the police off to prevent them from getting too excited about the sex in the club, and as I seemed to be putting my face about a bit, I just guess he got some kind of two-for-one deal: protection for the club with me not getting sent back home thrown in.

It didn't take all that long for the lifestyle to catch up. I was shoving more and more coke up my hooter and surviving on less and less sleep. I'd go for days without getting more than an hour or two here and there, all the time keeping myself topped up with charlie. I'd become so dependent on it that snorting seemed to take too long for the effects to come on, so before I DJed I'd roll about 10 coke smokes: take the tobacco out of a normal ciga-rette, mix it in with some charlie, shove it back in and rip out the filter, which I'd bite in half and shove back in. The hit was instant, but the comedown was the worst.

I began to see the world through different eyes. Now I'd admit that they were the bloodshot red berries of the addict, but back then, well, I suppose I just thought I was encountering the inevitable lows that followed the sweet-tasting highs. It didn't occur that it was a problem, just a payment.

Anyway, I began to notice that loads of the other people working at The Bahamas were similarly off their faces. The barmen had that same vacant expression, the one that made them look like really bad actors. They were unable to play the part of 'normal bloke' convincingly, and it was plain to see – through my eyes at least – that they were also getting the nod and the snort from the manager. I don't know how much he must have been pulling in, but it must have been serious cash if he was sorting the bar staff out as well.

Maybe I was a bit slow – I guess I just had my hands full with the coke and the decks and the onstage exploits – but after a while I began to notice various other things that were going on in the club. There was this group of girls, for instance, who'd turn up together every night and would each leave with a different smiling English lad as the club cleared. Now I could hardly say that I was a prude, but to keep that sort of turnover up for weeks on end eventually got me thinking, and I asked my mate, the other DJ, Sidro Perez, what the score was. I wondered if they were prostitutes. Sidro laughed and told me they were men with a taste for unsuspecting giddies. They'd take them wherever they'd take them, do whatever they'd do to them and come back the next night for more prey.

Of course it was none of my business, but at first – as a young lad from Wythenshawe – I was pretty wide-eyed about the whole thing. I was amazed that people were falling for it, but I suppose I'd been taken in myself too. I imagine that some never found out, while most people went home with their tail between their legs, desperate to forget all about it. Some obviously felt the need to get in touch with their anger there and then, and occasionally you'd see the trannies come in with black eyes and the odd missing tooth. Funny, that, as their injuries always seemed to be facial. Must have been a desire of the 'victim' to warn others away from their mock-femininity.

Coke

So, we're almost at the end of my first season at The Bahamas. I'd not given much thought to what might happen when things closed down and the giddy pound was no longer being flashed around, but at the very least I knew the season had a few more weeks to run and I was safe for that long at least. I was wrong. One day I turned up for work, expecting the usual ritual of the nod and the wink to join the boss in his office for a 'chat'. But there was no José Carlos, no nod, no wink and consequently absolutely no charlie. Now, five months of plentiful powder had not left me in an ideal state to cope with this sort of hiccup. I went ape.

'Pedro' – one of the local barmen – 'Pedro, you've absolutely got to help me out and take me somewhere I can score right now, Pedro.'

'You see,' he shrugged, 'there just isn't any. José Carlos's away in Madrid but even there nobody's got any.'

That was not what I wanted to hear. That was not what I wanted to hear at all. I retreated to the toilet where, sweating and shaking, I wondered whether there was any way that I might get through the next 18 hours. No was the answer: there was no way that I could get up on stage in front of 2,000 people and lead them in having a mad one. There was no way that I could go on to Black Sabbad and throw myself into the anthems and the tunes, providing a soundtrack for the day trippers from the propaganda crews. I went back to Pedro and pleaded.

'You've got to help me, Pedro. I'll take anything just as long as it's enough to get me out of my head for the night.'

He took pity on me and took me outside to his motorbike. I climbed on the back and went with him into the old town to get some gear. He was in a rush as he had to work that night too, so there was no time for a commentary on where we were going or who we were going to be dealing with. We wound up in a place I'd never been before, somewhere with loads of railway arches and all that. It was seedy to say the least, and Pedro pulled over and got off the bike. I went to do likewise but he stopped me.

'No, no. You can't deal with these people. Just stay there.'

Well, that felt wrong for a start. I never liked buying at the best of times, but when I did and it was from a stranger I always made sure I saw what was going on. But my desperation made me sit down, play dumb and wait for Pedro to do the deal.

He'd gone over to talk to a couple of lads. I watched them chat, and after a little bit he handed over the cash and they gave him what I thought must have been a cellophane-wrapped palmful of charlie. It was a result and I was happy. Still, time was running out so we put our celebrations on hold and legged it back to the club.

We headed straight for the basement, sat down among Andreas's literature and crusty sheets and got straight down to business. Pedro started pulling things out of his pocket but I was still shuddering from my memory of staying down there with the pint- puller a few months before, and hardly noticed what Pedro was doing. When I couldn't see any of the usual lining-up going on I took another look: he'd pulled out some tinfoil and a small container. He snapped the top off and was pouring this brown liquid onto the foil. He had a bog-roll holder which he stuck in his mouth, held over the foil which he lit from beneath and started inhaling. Me being a bit green still and never having seen heroin before, I thought this must have been some new kind of liquid charlie. So with two and two just not adding up to anything like four, I took the foil when he gave it me, watched him put some more liquid in, hold his lighter beneath and started breathing in the fumes that came off. I felt a bit stupid with the bog-roll holder in my mouth, and for a while I was just left feeling confused. What was it? An upper or a downer? I didn't know what to expect until all of a sudden I started feeling sick. This, I was telling myself, was not nice. I didn't like it, and especially not when I started feeling all floppy as well. I was just about due on stage, screaming and shouting in front of 2,000 people, and all I felt like doing was curling up and having a kip. It was crap.

I stumbled out of the basement, made it to the DJ box and had one thought. I can't handle this. I started feeling sick again, and this time I puked. After that the rush that hit me was even worse, and it was about all I could do to get Sidro over and tell him to take over. I got out of the booth, went back to the apartment and lay on top of the bed, sweating and feeling less high than I had done in a long, long time. I whipped my clothes off and lay there stretching. The whole bed felt like a marshmallow and the beads of sweat were like ice cubes.

I must have liked it a bit as I took it again. Like a good salesman, Pedro believed in his favoured product, and he told me that the first time always left you feeling sick. If I kept going with it, I was told, I'd be OK. And I was. Over the next year or two I used it more often, but never injected it. That was always my line in the sand, and as long as I never stuck a needle in my arm I knew I didn't have a drug problem. Everyone I've ever met seems to have a similar outlook, with some kind of boundary acting as a definitive line: if you're on the right side then you're home free, no problem or nothing. But if you cross it, you're screwed. Unless you shift the line, which of course we all do when it suits us.

All those things you've heard about the coastline of mainland Spain – that famous Triple S cocktail of sun, sex and sangria – well, they're all true. As I've said, I was doing my bit to keep it real from the stage, not something I'm proud of, but I was also keeping the big monster called loneliness away by hooking up with some new Cindy, Sarah or Sue every week. They weren't exactly deep and meaningful, and it contributed to an atmosphere of general secrecy: it felt as if people were hiding things, only showing as little of themselves as they could get away with.

Take my mate Shane, for example. He was one of the many prop lads who were on the run from the police back home. He was into fraud and all that, and Alicante was like heaven on earth. His mates back home would nick credit cards and then send them out to him the next day. Shane would go on a manic 24-hour spending spree, safe in the knowledge that it would take at least a couple of days before there would be a stop placed on the card down in Spain. As fast as he bought the gear he'd sell it dirt cheap, and I guess he split the profit with his mates back home in dear old Blighty. How did I know this? It was only because he was a rabid amphetamine fiend that I found out. As long as I knew him he was fond of injecting amphetamines, and it hadn't done him any favours.

He'd got in with the local drug big boys, and from time to time used to sell a bit of gear or whatever for them. At other times he was working his own scams and generally keeping himself in needles and wizz, but inevitably he lost his balance and started to owe more than he had. I'd lend him cash now and then – I just liked him and his girlfriend, I guess – so I was made up for him when he came into the club one night and told me that he was going to be able to pay off all the money he owed me as of the next day. He told me that he had to do a run to Madrid and back, carrying coke and weed for whoever. I don't know why he told me – perhaps he wanted reassurance – and I told him to give it a go. Not quite my scene, but he seemed pretty keen himself and he did need the cash.

Anyway, it turns out that Shane was a bit on the nervous side. In fact, he'd got so stressed that in an effort to make himself calm down, he'd smoked his way through a considerable amount of hash. It did the trick, although it did it a little too well as it happens. The story goes that he was driving along in one of those beach cars made out of corrugated iron, I think they're called Mooks, and was so caned that he must have fallen asleep. Anyway, he ended up drifting under an articulated lorry, slammed on his brakes and wound up with the lorry driving right over and killing him.

Thinking about death, there was this barman who worked at La Pollo. It was the kind of bar where all the workers would go to hang out and take it easy.

Simon was one of the soundest blokes I'd met out there, and loads of us felt the same way. So we were all pleased for him when one day he wheeled his new motorbike round the front. There was all the usual chat and he got on it to show us what it could do. He was only going about 15 miles per hour down the street – hardly even warmed up – when a car pulled out of a side road and Simon went over the top. He died instantly and the whole bar looked on in utter shock.

His death did something to all of us. We held a night to try and raise enough money to send his body back home, and there were all sorts of people turned out; alkies, junkies, dealers, blaggers, crims and scallies. I think it made some confront the fact that even though they may have believed otherwise, they hadn't really escaped the situations back home. A few people packed up soon after and went back to face whatever music was waiting for them.

It's the end of the season. What next, eh? Simon's death was too much, a smack in the face from reality, one that neither of us wanted. I thought Spain was supposed to be a place of escape, somewhere I could come to avoid all that cack from back home. Do I pack up and leave like the others? Not me. I'm sticking it out here. It may have put me through my fair share of grief and confusion, but facing the consequences of battering one of Manchester's main men is just something that I'm not up for contemplating. But why Simon? Why him? Where was the fairness in that? He deserved nothing like that, had never done anything wrong, never stole, hated, hurt or whatever, so why should he die? I'm not taking that, I'm not letting that happen to me. I'm not going home to face Wythenshawe and I'm not going to let death get me out here either. It might come later but for now I'm living for the man, for the moment. Come on!

But that fades. The hype eventually dies down and I'm left with an eternal WHY? hanging over my head. Simon's death. Why? It makes no sense, but even confusion fails to make me feel better. I hate these loose ends.

FEAR

Alicante was my Ibiza. While the London set were just beginning to make their way to San Antonio, there were plenty of us –
mainly northern – scallies creating our own hedonistic fantasy,
blissfully unaware that something kind of similar was going on in
the middle of the sea. Of course, in time we all got to hear about
it, and eventually I made my way there too, but if that first
season in Alicante proved anything, it was that if you give people
enough drugs, enough reasons not to want to go home and
enough gentle corruption, anything can happen.

So anyway, the season finished some time towards the end of
September, and as expected the exodus of the tourists made for
a pretty swift change throughout the place. Suddenly the jobs
just weren't there, and the propaganda lads were the ones to
feel it first. They never had much of an opportunity to save
when they were only on a tenner a night, so within a few days
of the clubs scaling down their operations, plenty of their
External Marketing and Promotions Executives packed up and
moved on. But some stayed back, which was good. I'd managed
to put some money by, and wound up renting out a big villa. The

lads moved in, and we settled down for a winter season of continued excess.

Of course, the tourists may have gone but the locals were still there, still wanting drugs, clubs and whatever else took their fancy. This meant that there was money to be made – although considerably less than from the sunburnt Brits – and fun to be had. The villa was just over the road from a rocking club called Penelope's. It was the absolute dog's Balearics: swimming pools and palm trees, naked nymphs and hardcore nutters. Actually, that's a lie: there were no natural hardcore fiends among the locals, or certainly there weren't enough of them to inject that all-important spice into a club. So when we all turned up, the response was similar to that which we got in Black Sabbad: come in but stay in the corner. It's not that they didn't like us – we all got on well – but to the Spanish, we were true giddies: getting excited about every little thing. We'd all climb up on a bit of staging – 50 or 60 of us – tripping and speeding for all our worth, and just have a full-on mad one. It was all harmless fun, but we knew our place – sweating on the stage in a big group, a minor attraction that was harmless if left alone.

Life settled down pretty quick. I still DJed in The Bahamas, but only at weekends. The prop lads would make ends meet by doing whatever they could. I'd been feeling pretty rich when I'd taken out the lease on the villa, and had paid five months up front. For the first month I just assumed that I had no money worries at all, until one day I happened to find out that I had about as much money in the bank as I did when I arrived. My drugs consumption must have taken a big bite out of the pile, especially as I'd been getting nothing for free. It was a worry, but at least I wasn't alone. I was back to how things were in the early days, and to keep us in food, we'd all go on raiding parties during the night. Our favourite was the local mango farm. Very nice they were too, but not after six weeks.

Fear

Of course, like anyone who opens the door to drug excess, I regretted it. Frequently. I've lost count of the number of times I threw grams of coke in the bin, declared tomorrow a new day and swore never to touch the stuff again. Probably the one that I believed in the most happened about now. I was used to coming home from work at night to find my fellow tenants chopping up lines on the table, but somehow this one night things were different. As usual I'd necked half a bottle of whisky during the night, and I'd only managed a handful of hours' sleep during the previous few days. I needed to lie down and not get up for a long time, but the lads were having none of it.

They were particularly excited because of some new skunk they were smoking. I'd never been one for the spliff – I always preferred to go up rather than down – but this time I just went along with the rest of them. I don't even know how strong it was, but it must have done something to me as within minutes I was rushing like a master. My head was going ballistic from the coke and weed, and I needed to get out. I went outside and swore at the stars for not being close enough that I could grab them. I went back in. More coke. More weed. Then came the trips. I hate trips. I've never really gone in for them, but somehow there was no backing out of it. Someone had put some tunes on, they were calling it Belgian New Beat, and I spent what seemed like an eternity wondering how they were spelling 'new': were they going for the established correctness of NEW or the slightly edgy, futuristic nature of NU? I couldn't decide and the debate raged on within my mind. There was a strip of trips on the table, and for some reason I wasn't content with just necking one, I had to lick the whole darn strip, back and front.

I stood up. The trips came on and I'd had enough. I was angry at all these people for being in my villa, and I needed to get out. So I went for a ride on my moped, weaving around the town for hours on end. Getting caught by the police would have been a bad idea, so I tried not to draw attention to myself. Having said that, I probably looked about as subtle as a beached whale, driving along at 17 kilometres per hour, alternating between swearing at the sky and shouting about mangos.

I wound up on a bit of scrub land outside the town as the sun was coming up. I repeated the 'never again' phrase over and over, hoping my mantra would make itself real. I went to sleep on a rock.

I woke up and the sun had risen. My watch told me that it had also set as well, and I'd been out for something like 24 hours. This was not good, as 24 hours meant that I'd missed my slot at The Bahamas. I got back on my bike and headed for La Pollo. It didn't take long to work out that I was in trouble, that José Carlos was going to have a go and that I might be sensible to start looking for other work.

I went to see him as soon as I'd plucked up enough courage, and sure enough, he wasn't happy. The worst thing was that he wasn't angry – at least he didn't shout or break things like I'd seen him do before. Instead he told me the score much as you'd read out a recipe.

'You are not taking the piss out of me. You do this again you have no more free coke. You have no more job. You will never leave Spain.'

I didn't ask how exactly he was thinking of making that last bit happen, but he seemed upset enough to be taken seriously.

'I want you at The Bahamas at the right time every night. I want you happy and your head to be sorting it out. Otherwise you're finished.' It was a pretty persuasive argument, and I agreed to sort it out. So much for giving up drugs, and I knew full well that while 'sorting it out' meant no more repeats of the previous 36 hours, it also meant keeping myself nicely charlied-up for the punters.

I settled down and soon had myself convinced that I was handling it. Like all my friends, I'd built up a huge back catalogue of thoughts about drugs: why I did them, why I liked them, how long I'd take them for and why I didn't have any sort of problem. Even after the incident with the trips and the weed, I was still able to deny any suggestion that things were less than perfect. As far as I was concerned, as long as I wasn't digging myself, as long as I stayed away from the needles, then I was purely a recreational drug user, nothing more. As I say, all my mates were similar, drawing their own lines in the sand and declaring themselves fully fit and problem free as long as they were on the right side of it.

I had to adjust my own personal line every now and then, especially when encountering new drugs. One night some prop lad was banging on about a new high unlike any he'd ever experienced before. He called it Happy and like all good home-made highs, there was a complex ritual surrounding the preparation. It started with a packet of diet pills. Crushing a whole packet up, the resulting mound of powder was placed in a tapestry of Rizlas. The whole thing was then folded up into a neat (but not so little) parcel, and swallowed. As soon as it had passed the gob you'd have to neck a can of Coke.

I was due at work an hour later, and aside from feeling like I'd just swallowed Dick Whittington's bundle, I forgot about Happy, and carried on with my life. And it was fine, until I reached the DJ booth. There were two spotlights above the decks and the shafts of light stood out clearly amid all the dry ice and smoke. It was a pretty little sight, until I went to put a record on. The minute my hand passed under the light an agonizing pain shot through my body. It was as if I'd just been burned with acid, and the only explanation I can give is that it must have either sensitized my skin or altered my perception, which, let's face it, is probably the most likely explanation.

The light seemed to be almost burning me, so I was trying to avoid getting near it. That made putting records on the turntable quite difficult, which is a shame as being able to put a record on the deck is one of the more basic elements of DJing. This was not good news. It had only been a few weeks since my telling-off, and I was really starting to worry. I didn't think to get the lights turned off, and instead called over one of the barmen to come and help. For the rest of the night I'd shout out which record to put on next, and he'd whack them on. There was no mixing or anything flash, just back to back (well, almost).

What happened towards the end of that night is hard to explain. I started to yawn. It was a good yawn, nice and long, slow motion too. But my jaw locked. I couldn't shut it and all I was able to do was look about me. The barman was loving it as he was getting to be the DJ, having long since given up on following my instructions about what track to play next. José Carlos was staring daggers at me, probably wondering how long it would be before he'd end up giving me the boot. The punters were busy getting lost in their little alcohol-sculpted universe, shaped by the sounds of Madchester's finest. This yawn still going on, I started to stretch. From standing with my fists by my chest to reaching a point where my arms were outstretched must have taken almost three minutes. That's some stretch, and it was accompanied by pins and needles throughout my body. I just couldn't stop, and the only thing that was going through my mind was what a badly named drug this was.

I got home somehow (being dragged by some mates, I think), and spent the rest of the night and the following day lying on the villa's roof garden. My mates kept on bringing me Cokes to drink, which was about the dumbest thing I could have drunk as all the caffeine in them kept me up. I had to go back and DJ for the next two nights, still aching with pins and needles, still stretching and yawning like a complete weirdo. That, and I'm sure you won't find this surprising, was the last time I tried Happy. I'm sure it was just someone who was either bored or skint, looking for some cheap laughs or ready cash. I suppose they got what they wanted, but I never heard anything about it after that.

It was clear that the winter wasn't going to be much fun: too few drugs and too little cash. I wanted out – at least for the season – so that I could at least carry on the buzz elsewhere. I decided to go with the truth:

'Listen, José Carlos,' I said one night before I was due on. 'My gran's died and I have to get home for the funeral.' While he didn't exactly open up the old floodgates of sympathy, José Carlos wasn't that fussed about me heading off for a bit – I think he'd had enough of my antics over the previous few weeks, and probably he was guessing that I wouldn't come back. Of course I did, but not until after a handful of eventful encounters back home.

Having scraped together enough cash to get back to Manchester, I left as soon as I could. My journey out to Spain had been a bit of an epic, but a cheap one nevertheless. This time round I blew a couple of hundred quid on a flight and two taxis. I didn't have the money to waste but something was drawing me back home faster than I'd have thought possible.

I got the cab to take me straight to my parents'. I'd phoned them from the airport and told them I'd be round in an hour, but walking up to the front door was stranger than expected. They'd moved house and I knew no one would know where to, but it didn't stop me from feeling uneasy about seeing them again. Maybe it was all to do with the fact that they'd moved, but everything seemed different. They looked older, and while they seemed happy to see me, I could tell they were worried about what I'd been up to. I'd been speaking to them on and off throughout the year, so it wasn't like it was a big shock when I told them some of the things I'd been doing (clubs and DJing that is, not the coke and smack). Still, I think I'd managed to forget just what things had been like when I'd left. So much had happened to me over the year – from holding down a job and getting my own place to getting off my face on charlie as often as I could and standing in front of a club full of people each night – but to my mum I was still the little boy that left after he'd split up with his girlfriend. There was a lot of catching up to do, and Mum was pressing me for more info, but there was no way – I wasn't going to tell my mum about my adventures. After an hour or so she gave up the inquisition, so I just settled back and let things carry on the way she thought they were.

I'd spoken to Vinny, and on the first night out we were planning a large one to get me back into the swing of things, Manchester style. But there was a problem: while in Spain all I'd been hearing was 'HaciendaEcstasyHaciendaEcstasy'. It sounded like the best thing ever, but Vinny confirmed my thoughts: it was full of Manchester madheads. Now I was hoping that things might have calmed down a bit while I'd been away, that Darren might not be calling for my head on a plate, but I didn't want to take too many risks. Sadly The Hacienda was too dangerous, so we scaled our plans down a bit.

Vinny and I headed for a little club called Time. I managed half the promise, though, and wedged a couple of Es down my neck. My first times on any drugs have always been worth remembering, and E was no different. Despite the fact that it seemed to take an eternity to come up – especially compared to the rate at which charlie got out the blocks – when those whole-body rushes came on I was high 'n' happy like never before. What can I say about it that hasn't been said before? It was never in danger of being done under the Trades Descriptions Act. I soon was as happy as Larry, although I was quite possibly the only person buying any drinks from the bar. Old habits die hard, but young ones can take quite a kicking too, and there was no way that I was going out without a few fistfuls of whisky.

It was a mad night – a total mishmash of weird people: baggies, aceeed fans, even a few 'alternative' types. It wasn't so much dancing as punching the air. I was getting higher and higher on the rushes when I felt a tinkling on the back of my neck. By the time I realized that I'd had a glass broken over me I was tumbling through the crowd towards a door. I didn't know who was behind me, or not until I managed to turn my head and catch a glimpse of someone I really didn't want to see. It was Darren, and he was nowhere near as warm and cosy as I'd been feeling up till then. He was a hard man, and had received a call from a mate who had seen me in the club. Darren had legged it down to Time with a few of his heavies, with the intention of sorting out a little unfinished business.

Darren's lads were trying to force me out onto the street but the bouncers obviously didn't want anything going off inside their venue. I knew if they got me outside that I'd be dead or closer to it than I'd like, but somehow, one of the staff managed to get between me and the heavies, shoving me into a room. I didn't need to be told to run, and I slammed the bars down on the fire door at the end and ran as fast as I could away from there.

Now it's one thing to run for your life when you've got a straight head, but when you've got a couple of White Doves tickling up your nervous system, it's another matter altogether. Oh yeah, and when they're inside you for the very first time ... that's another matter altogether. Every noise or reflection of light had my panic levels climbing even higher, and I can remember crouching under a bush, shivering and wishing things were different. I knew they knew where I lived before, and it made sense that they'd want to finish things off now. I knew the way it worked; getting potted in Time was not a warning, it was no sign that I could relax having got away with a close brush. Now there was even more unfinished business on the menu and they would never let it go without a fight. I went back to my parents', picked up my bag which I hadn't had time to empty, and made my way over to Vinny's. Why Vinny's, I don't know. It was safer at my mum's, but with all the pressure on me, being with a mate was worth trading in on a little of that safety.

I spent the next few weeks keeping my head down. Vinny lived on Barmby Street, in the centre of Wythenshawe, and I generally didn't stray too far from his flat. There wasn't much going on, but at least it was safe enough and I could talk things through with him when I wanted. I'd split my time between sleeping or watching telly inside and going out to the pub or the market.

I was there one day, flicking through a record stall, wondering if there was any way that I could mix in anything from *The Best Of James Galway* with some of those fat little tunes I'd been hearing since I got back.

'It *is* you!' came a voice that was accompanied by a hand tugging at my jacket. I turned around and clocked the girl who was talking to me.

'Don't you remember me? From The Bahamas, that club in Alicante?'

My mind had completely dislocated itself from the situation. Anyone who recognized me was a potential threat, and even though I knew she was probably safe, I started to get worried.

'... I had the best time out there we only went for a week but I stayed for two and we came to The Bahamas every night and do you remember getting off with my mate Sarah she remembers you and she'll go mad when I tell her that I've seen you and what are you doing here now and do you live here and are you going out ag—'

Suddenly I could see her lips moving but I could hear nothing. I was in my own world, isolated, and the pressure started to rise. Like butterflies in the stomach, I was feeling overwhelmed by waves of panic. I was convinced that she could see my insides, as if my body had flipped inside-out and all my organs were there on show.

96

Fear

'Icanttalknowimreallybusyivegottogo,' I blurted out, running away from her until I found a quiet place to stop, at the back of a parade of shops. There I squatted down, holding my head and desperately hoping that the feelings might go away soon. I felt worse than I'd ever felt before, and I hadn't taken a thing. I knew I needed to get home and have a lie down. I did that, and within a few hours felt better, but it was not the sort of better I was hoping for. The racing heart and the extreme nervousness passed, but a low-level sense of fear remained. I was worried, unable to settle and I didn't like the way things had changed. Eventually, after a few days, I was back to normal, but the feelings would come back every so often, usually after a big night out.

The episodes were freaking me out as they were coming on more and more frequently. I suppose it was all to do with living with the fear of getting caught all the time, but then again, the drug intake can't exactly have helped with my mental balance. It wasn't long before my mind returned to happier times, and I started thinking about what else I could do to stop these bouts of panic. Spain was the only answer I needed. I knew that was where I was happy, the place I was meant to be. It wasn't just the drugs, the clubs, the weather or the fringe benefits. Actually it was, and I was missing it like one lover misses another.

I didn't stay away from the shops completely though, and one day me and Vinny's brother Billy were walking along. At the other end, a hundred yards away, I saw Trisha, Darren and a pram with two kids in it. Somehow they kept walking towards us and me and Billy carried on too. I don't know what I was thinking, but whatever it was it wasn't clever. I recognized Trisha's first kid in the pram, but the other was just a baby. I wanted to see if I could recognize myself in it. Before I knew it, we had stopped a couple of yards apart and Darren had squared up to me. My dad had always taught me to get that first punch in if it looked like one was coming, and as soon as I could I headbutted Darren full on

97

between the eyes. He went down and I was amazed. All this stuff that surrounded him, all this stuff about his family and all that, it didn't count for nothing. He got up and I didn't wait to be asked. I punched him as hard as I could and again, he hit the floor. I wasn't going to hang around to see if he got up again so it was time to run. Billy and I legged it, and the next thing I knew I heard a shout from behind and turned to see Darren chuck a bottle after us. It was a good shot too, but Billy stuck his hand out and caught it before it got me. He was cut up, but there was no sense stopping. We carried on running.

We've stopped. The dust has settled, we're free from Darren and my heart rate's come back down to something approaching normal. I've just rubbed salt in the wound and there is no way this is going to work out well if I stay around. I'm going back. Luckily I've lined myself up a job packing boxes in a warehouse. I didn't like the look of it when I went along yesterday, and even Spain isn't worth the aggro of nine-to-five. I'm going to jack it in soon after I start tomorrow, but not before I've sorted myself out. There are some seriously valuable electrical goods in that warehouse. I'm going home.

RUSHING

I'd felt nothing as I left Manchester, and I must have been saving all the emotion up for my return. I caught a flight to Barcelona and got the train back to Alicante. Arriving back there was like turning up at the pearly gates themselves. I was on cloud nine and everything seemed beautiful: the blue sky, the sandy beach and the scabby prop lads who'd been thieving their way through one of the coldest winters on record.

The season was starting up again with a few tourists kicking about. The Bahamas was up and running and José Carlos was kind of happy to have me back. He'd been busy in the four months that I'd been away, buying a plot of land next to the club and extending it. That meant that it could now house over 3,000 people, and he told me of his masterplan. He wanted to pull in not just the Brits but the Dutch and Germans too. That meant changing the music a bit, giving a bit more of a continental sound. I was just happy to be back and would have agreed to anything, but when he told me that he wanted to ease off on the Club 18-30 act for a while during the night, I was well happy. I'd been getting more and more into dance music and 'proper' clubbing, so much that getting people to shag on stage was losing its appeal. Still, the Catch-22 was in operation, as The Bahamas paid well – in both sorts of currency. A two- or three-hour decent slot in the middle of the night where I could try my hand at being a full-on DJ in front of a huge crowd was a definite plus point. Things were looking very good.

A few of us had christened ourselves The Chippie Lads. We were decked out head to toe in Chippie gear – the chinos, the tops, hats and all that – and were pretty much the only ones due to the price. We Chippie Lads were planning a recce over to Ibiza to see what all the fuss was about, and all I had to do was train someone up to take my place in the booth for the couple of weeks I was away. I had to pick the right person – not too good but not too bad – and so I was kind of interested when, hanging about in La Pollo, I bumped into the manager from a rival club who suggested we have a chat. I was thinking that he might be able to suggest someone, but he had other ideas.

He was one of those types of bloke that you're never quite sure what they're thinking. Sure, José Carlos was a bit of a shrewd businessman, but this bloke was something else. If he was English he'd be one of those hard bastards from Romford, all gold sovereigns, pit bulls and attitude. But in Spain they do things a little differently and this guy was modelling himself on an Italian mafia don. He was dressed in black, had dyed his greying hair black and wore black-rimmed shades. He was about two inches too big for his trousers, but even his spreading gut had a certain threatening air about it; maybe he used it to crush profit-stealing drug dealers.

I should never have been chatting to him, not that José Carlos was the jealous type, more that we all knew this guy was trouble. His club was a state and it was common knowledge that they hated the English and only wanted them for their money. What's more, violence was one of their main pastimes.

So anyway, we were having a chat; me and him with two of his black-wearing heavies adding an extra hint of danger to the proceedings.

'You should leave that place,' he said, waving a manicured hand in the direction of The Bahamas. 'You should come to my place instead.'

Not letting me reply, he carried on. 'I will give you more money, a nicer apartment and twice whatever it is that José Carlos puts up your nose.' He laughed at this, as did his monkeys standing either side of me.

'It's tempting,' I said, trying to work out how he was going to react to my full-on refusal, 'but José Carlos needs me over there.' It was stupid to assume that he'd fall for that kind of appeal to reason, but his smile told me that he was OK about it all.

'Oh, that's OK,' he said. 'I only want for you to be happy.'

Fair enough, I thought. He'd confused me with his niceness, but I still knew that he was trouble so I made my excuses and left as soon as I could.

Perhaps he had a bad couple of days or something, because when I next saw his two goons I paid for that no in full. It was a week later and I was leaving the club when I was jumped by three blokes. They grabbed me and took me off to the side of the club, next to an old swimming pool. I recognized the goons from before, but I also caught enough of a glimpse of the third bloke to figure out who he was too. He was called Binsie and he was a part-time policeman who, like all part-time policemen, was going through some informal police training on the doors of the local clubs. He was a bit good at his job and subsequently everyone kept their distance. A bit of distance would have been a good thing right then, as they tied me to a plastic chair. As usual I was off my head and finding the whole thing pretty freaky. At least, that was until Binsie took aim and punched me full on in the face. It felt like my nose exploded all across my head, and apart from wanting to get out of there, all I could think of was how it was hurting. They carried on, both having a good go at me, punching my face for a bit but then moving on to my stomach. It was not nice, and while I'd taken a few punches in my time before that, this was something special.

They were silent apart from one word, 'giddy'. Well, that could have applied to any one of a thousand blokes out there, and I started to think that it was a case of mistaken identity. Then Binsie said,

'You are one of the major drug dealers in Alicante.'

'Nah, mate,' I spat out as he seemed to be lining up for another punch. I tried to persuade him otherwise, that I was a pure lad who'd never touched so much as a Rizla. He wasn't having any of it.

'You going to jail,' he said next. He hit me again, this time on the jaw. My whole head felt like it was going to float away. But instead of concentrating on not floating away I hit back the only way I could. I'd always thought of him as being an idiot, and this proved it.

'You're just a doorman,' I said. 'You think you're the police but you're just a doorman. The Guardia wouldn't have you full time.'

That was a mistake, and Binsie pulled out a gun to prove it. That was it, I thought: game over. He showed it to me, telling me over and over that I was a dealer. Holding it up to my eyes, barrel first, he said,

'This is for you.'

The tears were rolling down my face as the two of them picked me up and threw me into the swimming pool. Was this it? Was I going to sink and drown? He'd said that the gun was for me, so were they going to get me out and then shoot me? I was confused, to say the least, and panicking like never before.

But this plastic chair I was on didn't sink. It floated back up to the surface and took me with it. I was bobbing sideways when the other bloke's boot came from the sky and pushed me back down. Back I came to the surface with just enough time to grab some air before the boot came back down and pushed me back. And so it went on, seemingly for ever. Inside I was crying for my mum, full of bitter remorse for all the things I'd done to hurt her.

They dragged me out eventually, and set to with some more slaps around my face. I gave up.

I came round a bit later on and they'd left me. I got home. I slept. I told José Carlos. I had a few days off. He was good about it and he knew that he needed to protect his investment, so there was always one of his bouncers around if I needed them. But things had changed. It had messed up my relationship with the rest of the clubs in the giddy part of town, and I could no longer go out where I pleased round there. I had to stay in The Bahamas, go to Black Sabbad or head out of town to Penelope's. It was not the way I wanted it, but I was changing too. It made me suspicious and insular, and I started only trusting a few people. It was just a few weeks that I'd been back, but already paradise was tainted.

So there I am, not in too good shape mentally, when I see Bob Slade – a Wythenshawe lad and mate of Darren's – in Alicante. IN ALICANTE? I was freaking out. It had never occurred to me to join the dots with the information that was gathering in front of my eyes: I'd got to know the guys who were selling most of the drugs to the Brits out there, and these dealers were all from Birmingham. I didn't wonder where they might be getting it from or whatever, I just thought they were all right for dealers. Anyway, I started seeing the sort of people around Alicante that I really didn't want to see. First up was Bob, whose brother was the boss's main man. I wasn't happy, and was convinced that he was over here to scout me out, to go back and tell the others where to find me so they could hand out the punishment that was surely coming my way. I tried to keep my head down, but he just kept on popping up: in a few bars, around town and finally in The Bahamas.

As the summer came along, all the Manchester heads turned up. I didn't know what to think: either they'd all come out to watch me get a good kicking (which was just a little too far-fetched even for my fevered mind) or by chance they'd happened to pick Alicante as the location for their summer of '89 sales conference. I didn't know what to think, but I ran out of time one afternoon when I came out of a bar and found myself staring straight at Bob.

'Arright?' he said.

'Ar-right?' said I, slowly.

'Eh, top one this Spanish lark! Come on!'

And that was it. He invited me back to the villa where he was staying, along with (as he told me) all the rest of them, Stevo included. I was freaking out, desperate to find out more, and convinced that I either got shot there in their villa, or later on. Get it out the way, I thought, so I went along.

It was all about business. There were a whole load of Brummies who had just started controlling much of the dealing in Alicante, but they were getting their stuff from and only oper-ating under the lads from Manchester. Manchester had allowed them to operate the Alicante drugs market like a McDonald's franchise. Bob's brother Mike was being left down there to make sure all was going smoothly and the rest of the crew were down to see for themselves. It was nothing to do with me at all and I felt just a little bit relieved.

I found all this out from them, and strangely no one seemed to be that fussed about killing me. They had lots of questions about how things were working and who was doing what. I told them what I knew and they seemed to find it useful. I was happy to oblige and all that, especially if it prevented me from getting killed. But I guess I just wasn't worth it, so I lived to fight another day.

Rushing

Mike and I became good mates. He even wound up staying in my apartment, and I'll always remember him as the bloke who could make me laugh unlike anyone else. There was one time in The Bahamas when I was playing some banging tune or other and Mike was giving it all he could on the podium. He was sweating and grinning like a true raver, when someone made a potentially fatal error: he tried to share Mike's podium. If there's one thing you don't do to a Manchester gang member while they're out off their face on charlie, it's share their podium. I watched Mike watching this young lad climb up there, only to receive a full-on scally headbutt the moment he stood up. The poor lad fell back to the floor, blood spewing out of his nose. Mike turned to me, stuck his thumb up in the air and carried on doing the frantically random arm-waving that I imagine he thought passed for dancing.

One morning at La Pollo he surprised me. He'd not looked up from his food for a while, and neither of us had said anything since we sat down. Not that that was unusual; mornings never have seen me at me best.

'Cam, I need you to know about something. I'm not going to make it for much longer like this.'

I was confused. 'What d'you mean? You're doing fine. We're doing fine, aren't we? We're having a laugh, aren't we?'

'No, not that. Not all this stuff. I'm fine with Spain. I'm fine with being out here. It's back home. It's all that. I can't keep going with it. I can't keep ...'

He trailed off as he looked up at me. I must have been staring pretty hard as he changed direction pretty quickly.

'Ah, don't mind me. It's just the comedown from the coke talking.' And we went back to our silence. What was all that about? It made me think, but no matter how hard I tried to get him to open up and talk about it again, he'd closed the subject completely.

A couple of years later I heard about a shooting in Wythenshawe. Mike had been in bed with his girlfriend and the two of them ended up dead. They found a gun. No one knows what happened, but a few think it was just a horrible accident, that maybe he shot her by mistake. Knowing how things would look and knowing how he'd go down with the law, Mike took what probably felt like the only option available to him.

I'd go with this theory myself, as I remember a few of the conversations he and I had together in the flat. Like Darren, Mike was a hard lad, but I don't think he ever really wanted to be where he was. I don't think he wanted the guns and the threat of death, and I don't think he wanted to be under other people all the time. In Spain he was free, more relaxed – he said – than back home. But back home called, and in a way it was probably a good thing – good for his health at least. You see, Mike had succumbed to the Spanish bug just like the rest of us: he'd become a right junky and his head needed some serious straightening out.

Mike stayed for a fair bit of the season, and his leaving got me thinking. I knew what was coming in Alicante: soon the punters would be leaving, the clubs would be shutting down during the week and the whole atmosphere would change. There would be no free drugs, not much in the way of wages and on the whole, little point in me hanging around. Having spent time with many of those Manchester heads had changed things too. I knew that I was pretty much OK, that even though Darren might be bearing a grudge, he didn't have the power that some of these other people I knew did. The chances of me winding up dead were considerably less than before, and while I'd probably still face a beating, it was worth the risk. I was going home.

But it was still a little early; the season wasn't quite over and there was still a bit of fun to be had. Luckily the rest of The Chippie Lads were on for doing a bit of an escape and checking out Ibiza. We'd all heard about it, but not so much from the point of view of something massive going on over there, but something underground. It suited us nicely and we threw in our respective jobs to go and pursue hedonism in a slightly different environment.

We weren't exactly rich, so we opted for the ferry that went from the mainland out to Ibiza. This also made us feel slightly easier about all the gear we were taking with us. We didn't know how long we were going to be there and none of us knew anyone out there. Like good scouts we were nicely prepared with a bag full of Es, a few grams of charlie and plenty of smoke. It seemed like loads but we all knew that the five of us could work our way through it in no time. The ferry ride was dull so we necked a couple of pills each and made our own entertainment. By the time we arrived we were buzzing nicely and somehow I got sepa-rated from the rest of the lads. They had walked off with the pills and the rest while I was left holding some of the weed. Even though I thought I was looking like a top lad, the police thought I was worth chatting to and pulled me over as I skipped my way off the ferry.

I guess walking out on my own must have looked a bit suspi-cious, and the police kicked off with the classic question:

'Are you here on business or for a holiday?'

I could handle that OK. 'Me? Oh, holiday all the way. I'm a party kind of guy and I'm just here to have some fun.' Shut up, Cameron. Now.

The holiday line didn't seem to wash with them and they took me to a room and sat me down. My Spanish was never that good and as they jabbered away between themselves I was at a loss to keep up. They were probably talking crap anyway, just making me feel nervous as the minutes passed by. Eventually they made me stand up to be frisked. I was all too aware that in my Chippie Lad turn-ups were a couple of parcels of weed, and they didn't have to be Sherlock Holmes to find them. Sure enough, it only took a couple of pats down there to reveal the stash, and once they had removed the weed the police just looked at each other, dead calm. I got put in the back of a car and driven off.

I didn't have a clue what was going on. I may have been a keen drug taker but I'd never studied around the subject that much. Years later I got given one of those Know Your Rights cards that tell the paranoid drug-related felon all he or she needs to know upon being invited in for a cosy chat with the Old Bill. That card stayed in my wallet for years, and I made sure I knew exactly what my rights were. But back in Ibiza, in that car, I was totally clueless. I had no idea what the penalty for possession was and even though it had fitted in my turn-ups, would the amount be put down as personal or dealing? I was bricking my load; one minute I had a picture of myself being taken to a deserted bit of the island to meet Binsie again for another game of drown the DJ, and the next I was sure they were going to dump me in a prison, leave me to rot and get abused by burly criminals who liked young lads from Manchester. Luckily I was wrong on both counts and we turned up at a large police station. I was signed in and an English-speaking officer joined me in an interview room.

He was nice enough and my mind turned to thoughts about getting away with a slapped wrist. I'd be out of there within a couple of hours and back with the lads in time for a large night out to celebrate my brush with the law. But this was classic good cop/bad cop stuff, and as the officer's questions focused in more detail on where I'd been living and what I'd been doing in Spain, my hopes of a swift release began to fade. Added to that was the thought that now we were split up and with no plans or accommodation booked there was little chance of meeting up again.

What started along the lines of 'How long are you planning on staying here?' soon became 'Where are you planning on selling your drugs? How have you got the rest of your drugs onto the island? Whose club are you going to sell them at? Who are you working for on the mainland?'

I was not happy. I'd given up trying to look calm and it was about all I could do to hold back the tears. I was put into a cell and left for a few hours. I gradually stopped worrying as the time edged on. In the place of the blind panic came an increasing amount of bitterness about the fact that my mates were free while I was banged up. Eventually the cell door opened and a new face came in. I was taken back to the interview room, but this time there was no sign of the English-speaking local cop. After I'd waited for 10 minutes on my own, the door opened and in came two cops who, judging by their uniforms, were from the Guardia Nationale. These boys were mean and were giving it all the Hollywood tough cop act; putting their face in mine, poking and shouting at me. They kept on asking me who I was working for, and just as there was no way I was going to be able to tell them that I had come over with some mates, I didn't want to drop them in it back at The Bahamas. I must have come over as totally suspicious, especially as I decided that silence was my only weapon. I sat there with my mouth zipped, saying nothing. Apart from keeping me and the others out of even more trouble it also wound up the plod. Result.

They kept me there for three days. They'd question me over and over, asking me who I was working for and all that. We were getting nowhere but I was beginning to feel sick. Eventually one of them burst into my cell one afternoon and told me to get out. No charges, no fine, no nothing. I guess the amount of weed I had on me wasn't that much after all, but I was too busy feeling wound up that they'd kept me there for so long to feel happy. Still, common sense set in eventually and I made my way out quietly enough and hitched over to the main part of Ibiza town. As I said, we'd made no plans, but we had talked about which clubs were supposed to be the best. My plan was to while away the rest of the afternoon before doing a tour of the clubs later on and hoping to catch up with them then. I was sat outside a café working my way through the last of my fags when Little Chippie Lee walked by. I couldn't believe my luck and ran out to grab him.

'Where are they?' he half whispered at me, looking wildly around.

'Who, Lee?'

'The cops. Where are they? Are you being watched?'

The poor lad had obviously taken a trip too many, leaving his head seriously messed up. It took a while to talk him down and convince him that neither was I being followed nor did my ciga- rette pack contain a tracking device. Eventually he agreed to take me to the rest of the Chippie crew, who were at a nearby bar. Little Lee had just popped out to buy some more fags and I was grateful that the rest of them didn't share his sense of paranoia. We got on with the job in hand and had ourselves a mad night to celebrate. The story of my incarceration got a few too many retellings, and I may have been guilty of polishing up the truth just a little for the lads. Still, they liked a good yarn and it made them happy to hear about their mate who withstood three days of the most extreme psychological torture, only to be released and praised for his ability to take what no man had ever withstood before.

The lads had scored themselves an apartment in Playa D'Enbossa and it wasn't exactly spacious. We were crammed in there and the only real option was to get outside onto the beach. While I'd been inside the lads had managed to get themselves some trips, and after a day out on the beach we went back to get charged up. I was dead keen on taking the trips and we settled down waiting for them to come up. Having skinned up for a while and tried to play cards but failed, the trips suddenly kicked in big time. The windows were open and the noise from the clubs and bars below was helping to make the trip a hectic one, probably a bit too hectic for Chippie Pete. We'd just come up when he backed out and said he was going to bed. With at least another five hours ahead of us and some celebrating to be done, I was not best pleased with this and followed Pete into the bedroom to try and talk him out. He was lying face down on the bed and no matter how many times I called his name he just wouldn't respond. Eventually the rest of the lads came and joined in the call for Pete to surface. It felt like hours were passing with us all leaning over him repeating his name. Finally he jumped up, screamed and ran out of the room to the balcony. We all thought he was going to do a Superman but he backed off and went out the door instead. He stayed out all night and although he was sane again when we next met up, things were never the same between the two of us. He blamed me for messing with his mind, and to be honest it was fair enough.

So, not a great start to the Summer of Love. We did manage to sort things out though, and started hitting the clubs. As it happens the places were pretty similar to those we'd been to on the outskirts of Alicante. Nights out began with excitement and ended in a daze, while the following days were spent recovering and all that. We got to know a propaganda guy named Carlos, a massive body-builder who had a knack for imitating English regional accents. One minute you'd be talking to a Geordie, the next a Scouser and then again a Spaniard. But his moods used to change as well and I'm sure it was all to do with the steroids he was taking to keep his physique pumped up.

It was Carlos who introduced us to Space, one of the most beautiful clubs I'd ever been in. It was stunning and we turned up there one morning at about 11. We'd only just woken up but the place was full of people who'd been going all night. It was a weird feeling; noticing the amazing atmosphere in the place yet not being able to join in. There people had been in heaven for hours and we were stone cold sober. So we sorted ourselves out, sat on the sofa and waited for things to kick off. And they did. The rest of the day was the ultimate, especially with the planes taking off and landing so near by.

Happiness had never come through jobs for me. Career was never an option and education had failed. Clubbing was something else. This was the bigger picture, the universal whole. It just got better. We all wanted to stay for longer but the fact that all our money had gone within a couple of weeks meant staying on in Ibiza was looking a bit dodgy. I phoned a mate called Malmo back in Alicante and asked him if he fancied coming out. He was an all-round shady type, and his speciality was credit-card scams. He said he'd just got a couple more cards in and fancied a trip and that he'd bring my records over. He was there the next day, punishing the credit cards and chilling out with us.

With Malmo and his borrowed cards as part of our crew the quality of life took a serious upturn. We hired some mopeds, bought some clothes and headed up for an afternoon in the mountains. Only trouble was that my biking skills left a bit to be desired and I ended up ripping too much skin off my legs and arms when I came off on a gravel drive. We spent time at Amnesia, Ku and all the others, dodging the American navy who wandered the island in packs and spent their time laughing at the rest of us English ravers all out there for the highs.

I managed to get a bit of work out there. It wasn't much, but it was a start. I'd got chatting with some string-pullers at Amnesia and had been offered a go: one hour at the start of the night. At first it was only one night each week and there were never many people on the floor, but I was off. This was what I wanted to do, this was what I wanted my future to look like. The rest of the time out there – seven weeks in all – became the typical blur of highs and more highs. The clubs blew my mind and the drugs seemed to open a door. This wasn't about going out, this wasn't about

112

having a laugh at the end of the day; this was the main and the only event that mattered. Standing in the middle of the vast dance floor in Ku on the last night there my mind took one of those snapshots that will stay around for ever.

So is this heaven? Is this the limit, the edge at which the eternal paradise begins? I'm feeling high but even that word doesn't do my state justice. I've gone beyond the physical, beyond the bit where it's about how I feel. I've reached some new kind of level. Looking down and my body's doing the dancing. Autopilot. I've got no say in what it does. It's drenched in sweat but it's still going. The only sign I'm getting that we're still connected is the background rush that's going up and down my spine, telling me that the E is still going strong. But it's more than that, more than the physical. More even than the music. I can't go on. I must go on. I will go on. My mind is in charge and I wonder if I'm just a spirit, a gas floating through these bones. Four Es in and a heart attack must be round the corner. Surely my body's going to go on strike, to take industrial action against this cruel master some-time soon. But even if it does, if this is where I'm heading, if this is the state I'm playing out eternity in, then fair enough. Fine by me. Just keep the rushes up and the people smiling and I'll be sorted.

ECSTASY

Perhaps I bottled it, but I got back to Manchester and stayed there for only a few days. I was skint again and there was nothing doing, so I hatched a plan to visit the Emerald Isle, land of my fathers and all that. After all that foreign living it was about time I got back to my roots. Who was I kidding? I wanted a little bit more time before I finally showed my face around town.

My Aunty Mary was skint too. She lived about 15 miles outside Dublin, had a large family and was a lovely woman. She would beg, steal and borrow to look after the family, and had her own struggles going on deep down. Her demons came at her through the drink, and it was that which killed her a few years back.

She was a wiry little woman and all she wanted to do was show people a good time. I turned up at her door unannounced, skint and without any plans. I didn't want to impose on her, but as soon as I arrived she turned on the hospitality.

'Ye've done what?' she asked me as she showed me into the front room.

'Just popped in, Mary,' I replied, lying. 'I've just popped in to say hello.'

Ecstasy

'Well, you just sit yeself down while I make ye some tea.'

I knew she was hard up, but she insisted on getting the food in and taking me out to the pub for a few drinks. She kept up like this for a week, but I could tell that she couldn't afford it. When I saw one evening that it was me who was getting the cooked meal and her who was having the leftovers I knew I'd taken advantage. I'd been there a week and announced that I had to go. It had only been a flying visit and I'd loved seeing her, I said, but I had to get back to England the next day.

I left in the morning and made my way into the centre of Dublin. I was back where I'd been two years ago, with just a rucksack stuffed with a few clothes, no money and nowhere to stay. I had no way of getting home but it made sense to head towards the docks. At least if I got there I might be able to get on board by blagging a ride with some truck driver or whatever. When I got to the docks at Dun Laoghaire it was raining and I'd been walking all afternoon. I couldn't face trying to run a blag at the time, so I found some arches, walked in under them and put my kit down.

'Well, Cam,' I told myself, 'you've really screwed up this time.'

It was one thing being homeless and stranded in Spain, but somehow Dublin in the pouring rain was a lot less exciting. The old breakdancing routines couldn't help me now, and the only way out was getting home. I just about had enough money for a phone call home, but what good would that do me? My mum and dad were skint too, so how could they help? My brother was the same and my only option was dossing down and trying to get some sleep.

I didn't get much that night, and things weren't exactly all rosy the next day. I was hungry, cold, tired, damp and starting to smell. My clothes felt mouldy and it was all in all a crap state of affairs to be in. Spain was a long way off right now. I walked back into the centre of town and ended up in the park near Trinity College. It was October but last night's rain had stopped and the sun was shining. People were sitting out on the benches eating

115

their lunch, and I swallowed my pride. I was desperate – hungry and dying for a hot drink – and walked up to people asking for 50p to buy a drink or something to eat. They were kind too, and after a couple of hours I was feeling better, with enough money in my pocket to buy a bag of chips or two and some tea. It hadn't even knocked my pride that much, come to think of it. It had been so easy to ask that I didn't think twice about going back the next day and doing the same. I'd sleep back in the arches and head into town around lunchtime. I'd come away with three or four quid, enough to keep me going for the day. I started meeting up with the dossers in the park too, talking with them about how they were doing and all that, keeping warm with a few swigs of whatever drink they shared with me.

Within a week I was in a state, but I kept on going. It would have been nearly three weeks that I stayed out there, kipping in the arches and begging for what I needed during the day. It went slowly at the time, but looking back now the memories are all part of one big numbed blur. I don't remember being either happy or sad, and I can't remember what made me snap out of it. Perhaps I'm kidding myself here, but I wonder if the weeks could easily have rolled into months. They probably could if I'd got into the alcohol, but for some reason I never really did.

But I didn't stick it out, and I did the only thing I could, headed back to Mary's. I walked all the way out there – 15 miles – and it took me all morning. I washed my face in a public toilet before I knocked on the door, and tried to do something with my hair. My clothes, well, they were a dead loss, but I made up some story about being on a mad round-Ireland trip, and that I'd just spent a few days camping in the north. It was just for one day, I told her, but could I come in and have a bath?

'Camping,' she said as she rushed me inside to the nearest comfortable seat. 'And will you be wanting some toast with your cup of tea?'

116

Ecstasy

She was an angel, filling me up with scran and washing my clothes. I had a bath, managed to borrow a couple of quid from her so I could get back into town, and stayed the night. The next morning I was in a different state altogether, and went back to the city centre looking for work. I was up for anything, anything at all, and found myself staring at the window of some Kentucky Fried Chicken place. There was a note saying that they wanted staff, and I walked in, put on a big smile and got to speak to the manager.

Ron was another English lad, but he was KFC through and through. If you cut him he'd probably have bled the Colonel's Special Sauce, and somehow I'd played it just right. I was that desperate I was trying really hard to seem keen, and I had prob- ably gone totally overboard. But Ron loved it, especially when I told him I could start there and then. He was chuffed that he had someone who was so keen to learn the ways of the Colonel, and I was desperate for a party bucket of chicken and chips on my first break.

I got trained and it all went well. At the end of the day I put on my best Loyal Employee smile and had a word with Ron.

''Ere, Ron. You don't think you could sub us a few quid on me wages? I'm a bit skint an' I did start straight away an' all.'

Ron loved it. 'Ah, I see what you're like, young lad. You're keen, uh? Not afraid to take risks, uh? Know what you want in life, uh? Probably be running the company before long, uh?'

I nodded on cue, and smiled as he said 'uh' many more times, thinking just one thought: 'Yeah, mate. Just give us the money.'

It worked though, he gave me 50 quid there and then and that was that. I went out, slept rough that night but got up first thing and found myself a cheap bedsit for the week. It took nearly all my money, but as I got free food at work I was laughing. I was back on my feet, sorted and that's about all there was to it. Nice.

Or at least it was nice until I got food poisoning. I'd been there a fortnight and Ron knew that I ate nothing other than party buckets with chips. I was like a canary down a coal mine, and if I went down with poisoning, it meant there could only be one food source to blame. But I was too ill to be thinking about this sort of thing, and I spent days chucking up in my bedsit, looking as green as they come. Of course Ron was concerned, but I get the feeling that he took a bit more care because of the special positioning of the place. His KFC happened to be underneath the national headquarters for the whole company. What happened on his watch was seen by the men in suits. No wonder he was keen. And no wonder he was worried. So he looked after me. He gave me sick pay, brought me Lucozade and told me not to worry about doctor's bills. He told me to get well soon and hurry back to work as there was a nice surprise waiting for me. I did and there was: promotion. I went from sweeping the floors to working the tills. I was on the up.

I also fancied a holiday. Oh well, I thought, it was at least worth trying the blag on. So I told them the truth about my breakdancing history. I think I even gave them a little demo in between the fryers. And then I got a little more creative with the truth. I told them that I was due to take part in a huge competition in Switzerland in a week's time. I told them it was a wonderful opportunity to represent not only England and Ireland, but the mighty Kentucky Fried Chicken as well. Of course, they would need to help out in some way: plane fare and spending money should just about do it.

I couldn't believe that they went for it. And boy, did they go for it: they came up with the cash as well as a specially designed outfit. It wasn't much more than a regular serving uniform, but it had extra logos and I could tell they'd put some effort into it. Bless 'em.

I turned up in Geneva with £300 in my pocket. It was nice enough I suppose, and I whiled away the time sitting about,

118

sleeping and congratulating myself on a top blag. I bought a bowl for a tenner but couldn't get it engraved, went back to Dublin with tales of victory, massive opportunities for KFC promotion and tears for the honour of representing so great an organization. They loved it and after a week I was gone, back to Manchester.

Ah, sweet Manchester. It gets a bit of a battering in the press and all that, and all right, it can be a bit rough, but it looked pretty good to me as I got home. Dublin had threatened to drag me down lower than I'd ever wanted to go, and the whole KFC thing felt all the more unreal because of it, like I'd switched straight from horror-flick nightmare to comedy caper. But I knew the clock was ticking and home was the inevitable next step.

Of course there were some serious forces pulling me back. Like Ecstasy. There seemed to be nowhere quite like Manchester for it, and I don't just mean the pills. It was all that other stuff that went with it: the music, the sense of being together and discovering something new, the idea that you were connected with a huge group of strangers. We knew Manchester was striding ahead, defining this new thing and that only served to make the buzz all the sweeter.

Now I don't want to get into a long and unhealthy rant about the demise, the capitalization of the club scene. I'll leave it for later, but if you were there yourself, you'll know that it's hard to look at things today and not wonder where it's all gone wrong. I can just about stop myself from launching into an 'it were grand in the good old days', but I tell you, it were grand in the good old days.

Anyway, I'd got back to Wythenshawe as I always knew I would. The situation with Darren had lost most of its steam, and I was pretty much free to do what I wanted, so long as I gave him space and didn't rub the hassle I'd caused him in his face. As I

119

like having two fully functional legs it wasn't too hard to comply, and for the first few days I felt as though I was letting out a huge sigh of relief. The Dublin story was a miniature version of the last two years of my life: being up against it, feeling like all was about to collapse, only to see things change massively overnight and wind up enjoying a top blag. But it was only now, as I felt I could relax in my home town, that I realized just how tense the last two years had made me. Spain may have been a laugh, but it was always an escape. Deep down I'm a hometown boy, and I think I never feel quite the same when I'm not near Manchester.

So what with all this unwinding, I was surprised that I wasn't happier. I was back home, safe and sound, and after a week or so of dossing about back at my mum's, I was just feeling tired. That's about it really, tired. I had a few quid to my name, not much, but it meant that I could do nothing for a few weeks. Maybe that was the problem; if I'd had to get out and graft right from the minute I got back then I might have stayed up. As it was I spent my time on the couch or out having a quiet one with Vinny. I'd have the odd spliff and that, but as far as charlie was concerned it was way out of my price bracket. For all my talk about Ecstasy and that I don't even think I was out clubbing every spare minute.

Although I'm not sure that I knew it at the time, the last two years of drug abuse had taken their toll. I'm not being all dramatic here, mind you, but I'm convinced that I'd spent enough time taking enough drugs that when I went through a period with far less of them fizzing around my body, I changed. When I was faced with the boredom of having nothing to do my whole persona changed. I felt that everyone owed me, that I deserved a break. If that meant staying on the couch all day then so be it. If that meant sponging off a relative, well, that was the score.

My brother was just 19 at the time, but he'd moved out and had got himself a little flat in Stockton Heath. He was working hard and pulling in enough of a wage from Maxell's Greetings

Cards to keep his head above water. Perhaps I was jealous that his start was so much more sure-footed than mine, but in keeping with the 'everyone owes me' philosophy that was kicking around my head at the time, I left the couch at my mum's and headed for the one at my brother's. It wasn't quite so comfortable, but to my way of thinking it was a decent change of scenery. I was paying him nothing in the way of rent and doing nothing about the house, but it all made perfect sense; he was my brother and, you guessed it, he owed me.

I suppose you'd have to say that I started to get a bit low. My brother was doing my head in and I was snapping at him more and more often. I'd taken to ordering him about, telling him exactly what I felt about him, his life and anything else that drifted across my mind during the long days spent in front of the box. And I had plenty to tell him. Of course what I really wanted to say was buried so deep down that it wasn't until years later that I sussed it out. He was out at work, and already setting up his own business. He was into office cleaning, and it was always clear that he'd make a success of it. I was dead jealous and couldn't stand to see him settled and happy.

Worse thing was that he was about to get married. He'd been going out with Trish (not my ex Trish, that is) for a while, and to both of them marriage was the logical next step. To me it was another excuse to get wound up, and even after they'd tied the knot I was still hanging around like a bad smell. I knew I was out of order, and not only because Trish told me. She knew she'd picked the better one of Michael and Veronica's two lads, and deep down I think I agreed.

I knew what I had to do, and I made sure I shook off the lethargy and picked myself up again. I'd missed it last year – too worried about Darren to try it – but things were different and this was one risk worth taking. I just couldn't hold off any longer. I'd been before during the breakdancing days, and the indie night just didn't seem to do it for me. This time I knew I'd love it, and I went on my own.

I'd got a trip off Vinny's sister as it just seemed like the right thing to do, seeing as how I couldn't get any coke at so short notice. Although I'd done the odd trip in my past, I'd never thought to combine it with dancing, so what with the fact that I'd heard so much about it and the vague threat from Darren, I was a bit nervous about the whole thing.

Walking in, all I could see were lights and shadows behind the thick plastic sheets that hung down from the ceiling. Pushing through it was like landing face down in the snow: the sight and sound was that immediate and unexpected. The black and yellow construction scheme wasn't bad, and the smoke, stage and DJ box right up high were nice touches too. It wasn't what I expected at all. I'd been in big clubs back in Spain, but they were just empty shells with a few palm trees dotted about. This was odd beyond description, and I think all I did for the four hours I was there was stand on the stage and shout 'ACEEEEEEEEEEEEED' at the top of my voice.

The only other club I'd been to in my home town was The Gallery, a Cheetham Hill club that was going when I was about 15. That was all hip hop, weed and the threat of violence. The Hacienda was the other extreme, with people dancing, smiling and laughing. It was something else, and while the size of the place reminded me of The Bahamas, I was especially glad when we got through the night without a wet T-shirt competition.

Inner City – 'Good Life', Black Box – 'Ride On Time', they were the tunes, and the whooping told anyone who was unsure that they were massive hits. Which of course they were. Even with the strange ones over on the left. They were the E heads, and the neon tubes that they spun around helped them stand out. They didn't dance that much, but they swayed from side to side, like the Bachalau boys back in Black Sabbad.

Ecstasy

When it was over I got outside and stood about, just savouring the dying moments before it was pumpkin time again. Someone shoved a note in my hand.

'Go to Affleck's Palace'.

It was handwritten, and in my state I was about ready to do whatever any random and anonymous handwritten note told me to do. Even if it told me to go to a shopping centre in the middle of Manchester at two in the morning. I moved around the people, holding my note to my chest.

'Are you going to Affleck's Palace?'

Nods in reply.

'Are you going to Affleck's Palace?'

More nodding.

'Are you going to Affleck's Palace?'

They all were, of course; who was going to disobey a command like that?

So off we went, walking the half-mile or so to Affleck's Palace. Why am I going to Affleck's Palace, I asked myself. I didn't know, but I kept on going, zombie-like, with all the others.

We got there but couldn't see anything much that was going on. We decided to have a look down the side of the building, and at the end, down a slope, there was a massive bloke standing by a door. We walked up and stood in front of the man.

'Five pound,' he barked.

I would have given him fifty, I was that scared. I handed him the fiver and he let me in. The others I'd got there with didn't come through the door immediately after me, so I found myself on my own in this labyrinth of corridors and fire doors under Affleck's Palace. At every door and on every corner was a handwritten sign saying 'This Way'.

The final corner took me face to face with a totally randomly flashing light, right at eye level. I walked by, and came out in this room that had the weirdest ceiling. It was about 10 foot high at

123

the entrance, sloping down to what felt like two foot at the other end. Bearing in mind the acid I'd taken I found this just a little bit confusing, but what with the note, the bloke on the door and the signs, I was in no mood to argue. I was simply doing as I was told, and if that meant crouching down like a gnome, then so be it.

The DJ was on the left, and there can only have been 30 of us in there, dancing away quite happily, but all the time with one eye out in case things decided to get any stranger, when suddenly the lights went up, the music stopped and the police steamed in.

'Everybody out!' screamed the officer in charge.

By this time I was doing well with my commands, so I just did as I was told and left the room, winding my way back down the corridors along with all the other punters and a few of the policemen. We were all hanging about outside, asking each other what was going on. We all felt the same about it:

'But I've paid my five pounds,' was the murmur that underpinned the air. I went up to one of the coppers and tried to explain it. If only they could see that it was a simple misunderstanding then we could go back in and get on with it.

'You see, the thing is that we've all paid, so it must have been legit. It was in Affleck's Palace so Affleck's Palace must have been OK with it. The man on the door told us to go in so we did. What was the problem, mate? Why don't you just let us back in?'

Somehow the coppers didn't see it quite the same way. Eventually we got the message and started drifting off. I waved down a black cab and headed home. The night had been so amazing, discovering this mad stuff going on in my home town, that I just couldn't stop myself from gabbing away to the cabby, screaming down his ear:

'IT'S AMAZING AIN'T IT MATE? DON'T YOU THINK IT'S AMAZING? I THINK IT'S AMAZING! ALL IS SO AMAZING

HAPPENING HERE AND I NEVER KNEW AND DON'T YOU THINK IT'S AMAZING?'

Not that it calmed me down, but I could tell from his eyes that the cabby was having second thoughts about me. Institution breakout was probably his main thought.

'AND THAT TUNE! THAT TUNE THAT WENT "AAAAAAAAAH, AAAAAAAAAAAH, HIIIIIIIIIIGHER" WASN'T THAT AMAZING? WASN'T THAT AMAZING?'

Well, at least I was happy. Getting in on the party scene pulled me out of the depression just enough to follow up a few old mates from Alicante. It's not surprising that when I told him I wanted to go to Birmingham my brother dug into his pocket to give us a few quid. I was off to see my old mates from Alicante, the ones who had been dealing the drugs to the tourists on behalf of the Manchester heads. I stayed with Brummie Carl, a top lad who made ends more than meet by selling Es. No prizes for guessing why it was his floor that I chose to kip on, but he was used to people trying to blag him for free gear. We got on well, and had some top nights out. Actually, we mainly had top nights in, as people would come round, I'd crack open my precious box of records and we'd all relive some of those heady moments from The Bahamas and Black Sabbad. 'Snappiness' by BBG, Adamski's 'NRG', 'LFO' by LFO, 'Expansions' by Elevation and the old N-Joi 'Anthem' were all the big favourites, and I still get a tingle down my spine when I hear Kaos's 'Definition of Love'. With a few of these sessions under my belt I could pretty soon feel the old Cameron returning.

But I couldn't live on my brother's handout forever, and painful as it was, I did what I had to do to get my hands on some ready cash. I sold my box of records back for a measly £200. It's painful to remember it even now – that box of tunes that had been all over Spain with me – but desperation is a cruel mistress.

Still, the money meant that I was in the running for a top

night out. Carl and his mates had heard about some new club that was happening in Stoke, just a few miles up the M6. We were keen all the way, but from the outside it looked like a dump. I didn't care how good they said it was, the venue, in my book, needed a bit of work. We had plenty of time to check out the outside of the venue too as we were queuing for hours. We'd heard that they were really hot on gear, so we'd necked our stuff just as we turned up, thinking that by the time we were coming up we'd be nicely inside the venue. Two hours into my first E and I was still outside, twitching away and telling anyone who'd listen that normally I wouldn't queue for anyone. But as it was Sasha inside, we all decided that it would be good to make an exception.

But of course once we were in we realized how wrong we'd been to even dream of criticizing the place. There was nothing about Shelly's that needed changing. The size of it struck me first; this big open expanse with a low ceiling, sparing lights and DJ booth away on the left. Next thing to hit me were the tunes. It was as if I'd walked into the biggest sonic fireworks display ever. It was like taking massive growth pills and suddenly turning into a giant. The tunes were huge, anthems that took you up just about as high as you could get, and then gave you a cheeky little grin and marched you on up a few more peaks.

It was like nothing else I'd been to before. Even more than in Ibiza, the minute you walked through the door there was a massive sense of community. Everyone was your mate and there was a sexual chemistry that was almost dripping off the walls. Even the dealers seemed to be up for it, dancing on top of the seats that ran all the way around the edge.

Here I am, back in the place I found last week. That was the first time ever at Shelly's but already I feel like the king here. I'm never moving from this place; second step in front of the DJ

126

booth. If there is a heaven then this has got to be the closest I'm ever going to get. It feels so deep, so spiritual that I never want to leave. Me and the Brummies are together: drenched in sweat, eyeballs twitching and sunk back into our heads. Our bodies are so sensitized that the merest contact sends me into a grinning, gibbering wreck. Some girl has just walked past me, brushing by my arm. My whole body's on fire. Icy fire. This is my church.

SORTED

I kept on going along to Shelly's through the next phase. The call of my home town could not be ignored, and I moved back after a few weeks with Carl and the lads. My brother had moved to Warrington in the meantime, and if that wasn't enough of a reason to move somewhere else I knew that I'd pushed it too far with him. I made my way back to Manchester. I was on the floor again, anywhere a friend would have me, but the weekly ritual of Shelly's on a Saturday night kept me going. Loads of us would pile down from Manchester, driving back at 3 a.m. and stopping off at Sandbach Services on the M6. The parties would kick off as two or three hundred of us would meet in the foyer, get some kind of sound system going and keep the party spirit going for just an hour or so more.

As the months went by the whole thing took on a life of its own. Suddenly photocopied magazines were getting passed around, and I'm sure that one of them featured a character who's now called Peanut Pete. Peanut Pete now has the honour of teaching children about the dangers of drug abuse, and I can only assume that he had some kind of conversion experience along the way. When I knew him he was a cartoon raver, E'd out of his skull. Each issue showed Pete getting up to a different adventure involving E, spliff, police and service stations. It was a top buzz, made slightly more enjoyable by the fact that it was normally read on E, smoking a spliff, watching the police scratch their heads and wonder how to deal with this mass of people at Sandbach Services who didn't really seem to be doing much wrong. Eventually Middle England won its war against us young evil junky baby-boiling scum and shut the services down just before we arrived every week.

One night the police moved us on but the vibe was most definitely still alive, and word soon spread that there was a party going on a few miles away in a warehouse in Winsford. So we went, all 300 of us. Bearing in mind that very few were in any sort of state to drive, let alone make their way to an isolated warehouse in an isolated town outside Manchester, it's a wonder we ever made it. It was all thanks to the miracle of the Dancing Indicators.

Let me explain. The only way of getting there was by following the person in front. But because the person in front may not have been the sort of person you wanted in front, you needed to have some way of knowing that they were with you. Usually four sweat-soaked heads nodding in time to a 4/4 beat was enough of a clue, but it wasn't always enough. So in came the Dancing Indicators: every minute or so if you were in the know you'd perform – two beats on the right, two beats on the left, a quick one on the right and two on the left, all done to a dum-dum-dum-dum-de-dum-dum-dum soundtrack. Pure genius or pure madness, I'm not sure.

We got there at about 4 a.m., the tunes were blaring and being among the first ones there, we thought we'd have a little pause, skin up and take another E. All of a sudden the dance floor clears as a Staffordshire bull terrier wanders in, half-dead chicken hanging from its jaws. The dog starts ripping it apart, flailing its head this way and that. I tell you, it was that violent it turned us all right off. The happy mood lifted and put a downer on the whole evening. Whoever it was owned the mutt wasn't doing anything about it, so we left, Dancing Indicators leading the way to some other car park or whatever.

It was because of Shelly's that I got into Bizarre Inc. Everyone had heard of them, and their massive tune 'Playing With Knives' was one of the first times I'd heard real quality techno mixed in with a truly uplifting vocal. Anyway, I was off my head as usual, gurning away, when this girl came up to me.

'How's it going?' she asked, her breath making my neck go ballistic. 'Are you on a good one?'

'Yeah,' I replied, grinning like a child at Christmas. She gave me a hug and it felt so good I actually managed to stand still for the duration. Not that there was anything unusual in that sort of thing; Shelly's was full of huggers every night. I was having trouble talking and standing at the same time so we went and sat down to chat, my legs and arms still bobbing along to the beat.

'Did you see my band on stage?'

I'd seen nothing all night except a lot of smiling people. My mind was a blank. All I knew was that the tunes had been banging all night and I was a happy lad.

She carried on: 'I'm a dancer with the band that were playing tonight. Have you heard of Bizarre Inc?'

That's nice, I thought, and went back to giving my full attention to the tunes. Just then another storming classic came on and merely bouncing my arms and legs was not enough to show my appreciation. I started rapping. Now, I'd rapped before a bit, but had never done it that seriously. I guess I was just out of my head enough not to care anything about what people thought of me, so I went for it. More enthusiasm than skill, but I went for it all the same.

'Ecstasy-you're-the-one-for-me-you're-my-fantasy-and-you're-taking-me-to-the-place-I'm-free ...' Like I said, more enthusiasm than skill. Or originality.

She called her mates from the band over and got them to have a listen. I was out of it and just enjoying the tune, but Andy, the band's main man, managed to make an impression on me. He looked like a typical raver; long blond hair in a ponytail, full scally, but with a hint of wisdom about him.

'Top one,' he muttered, chewing aggressively on his cheek as I rapped. He had the look of someone who was a long-term E taker, but it wasn't for a while that I found out he never went harder than the weed. Still, as I say, he looked the part and he sounded like a top bloke. I decided there and then that I could – and I would – trust him.

I met the others too, Carl, Dean and Angie Brown, and while I kept up the rapping they seemed to be impressed. They went off and it looked like nothing really was going to come out of it. Still, it was nice.

Shelly's was such a mecca for clubbers in that part of the North and Midlands, and from the beginning to the end it was dead busy. Some other club started up over the road from it (Entropy, I think it was called) and on the odd occasion we'd all go over to that one when we'd missed our chance at Shelly's. The likes of Mickey Finn were doing the honours, playing slightly harder stuff than Sasha's preferred vocal stompers, but it was a good buzz nevertheless.

It wasn't all happy times. The drugs sometimes threw up the odd surprise, and I can remember one night being hit by a particularly bad trip. I'd done about four Es, and even though I'd had the old rolling eyeball thing many times before, this occasion was worse than others. I felt like I couldn't see, and instead of pulling myself together, working through it and getting back up there, on this particular night nothing seemed to help. I couldn't concentrate and soon found myself having a bit of a panic. The best thing I thought I could do was go outside and get some fresh air. I felt a bit embarrassed doing it, after all, no one likes having to admit to a bouncer that they're a weak individual, do they? I could only have been in there an hour, and having paid my tenner to get in I made sure they'd let me back in when I was good and ready. I went out, sat on the bollards and got myself even more worked up. I couldn't see beyond how I felt that second, and there was nothing I could do to get myself sorted.

Some scouse girls, real sweaty Bettys in mini-skirts, came up to me. 'Youarright love?'

'I'm 'avin' a bad one,' I said, eyes bulging and rolling back.

'Com' 'ere den. Grab 'old,' they said and sandwiched me, two front and two behind. We started doing a conga around the car park, and by the end of it I was right up there, rushing again and feeling like I was back on top form. I went to go back into the club and the bloke told me that it would be another ten quid.

'But I told you I was coming back!'

'Yeah, I know,' he said. 'And I've just watched you sitting over there for the last few minutes. That'll be a tenner.'

I was that angry with him that the shock of it all brought me right back down again. Not a good night.

One night the after-Shelly's adventure took us back down to Birmingham, to a private party in a lock-up somewhere. It was about the size of a double garage, and there could only have been 150 of us there. It was about 4 a.m. and the tunes were showing no signs of slowing up. These were before the days when people realized that dehydration was a real risk when on E, and the emphasis was on keeping on going. We just didn't seem to think that the fact we were sweating buckets was a bad thing, it was more like the sign of a good time.

Sorted

So we're in this lock-up and things are going mental. It was one of those strange ones where everyone concentrated on their own moves and their own space. It was less of a huggy vibe and more of a hardcore endurance session. There was just one light, a strobe, and it was continually on. It was mad.

There was one lad there who I'd seen all night: he was rooted to the spot like the rest of us, pumping his arms and nodding his head, but he was giving it everything he had. He looked like he was totally out of it, and while others might occasionally catch a stranger's eye and give one of those head-up, eyebrows raised, exhaling smiles that says 'flippin' 'eck, this is a mad one', he was lost. Suddenly he collapsed and was on the floor. I'd seen people have a bad one and fall over before, but this was different, and the crowd that was gathering around him knew it too. He was twitching, as though going through an epileptic fit, and a couple of people were helping him out. Someone had their arm supporting his head while another was talking to him, trying to get his attention. The minutes moved on and he wasn't showing any signs of coming out of it. The party stopped. Someone called an ambulance which came and took him away. A couple of days later we heard that he'd died at the party.

Even though we were all about the same age, barely out of our teens, this one made us think. We realized that we were just flesh and blood, that we weren't going to always be guaranteed a safe trip. Living a full-on hedonistic life meant dealing with the consequences. Most of us are still trying to work out what they might be, but even back then we started putting two and two together. The creaky bones that greeted you the day after a big session put some questions in the mind. Not that we stopped doing it, you understand; it just meant that paradise wasn't quite as we'd thought.

Remember that girl I met in Shelly's the night I met Bizarre Inc? Well, I'd been seeing her for a few weeks after that first meeting, and we were getting on all right. It was nice enough that she was part of the band, but as I said, nothing looked like coming out of it so I put all thoughts of rapping for them again out of my mind.

They came back though. She called me.

'Eh, Cameron,' she said after we had got through the usual pleasantries of chat about Shelly's, tunes and weed. 'Remember how I told you about the MC we had in the band?'

No. 'Yeah?'

'We've got rid of him; he was too off his face on E all the time.'

Good lad!

'So we were thinking of asking you to step in.'

Ha! If only they knew. Still, I wasn't going to let their illusions get in the way of me having a top blag and I went along with the chat, letting them know I was interested.

Somehow I didn't think that anything much was going to come out of it. The band had done well with 'Playing With Knives', and they were a big enough name in the clubs. I thought they'd had their moment and never considered that they'd cross over into the charts. As far as I could tell the charts may have had a few acts filter through from underground scenes over the years, but they'd never accept the soundtracks to a thousand E-fuelled nights of hedonistic madness. Surely someone would twig and it was bound not to be allowed.

I got the call eventually. Now they'd got rid of the MC, it was time for me to try out. They must have been a bit suss about me as the gig I was invited along to was way up at what seemed like the top end of Scotland. But to my mind I had nothing to lose, so I pulled out my best party clothes, loaded myself up with wizz and set off on the eight-hour journey in my untaxed, uninsured grey Metro. The first bit of the drive was just dull and my mind was on other things, but as the scenery got duller and the day wore on I started to get excited about it all. It had been years since I'd been up on a stage with a mic in my hand. No, this was, if nothing else, going to be a laugh. I'd be up there, shouting at the crowd and getting off on the energy of the whole thing. It was bound to be a top night.

I turned up at the venue – an old cinema – and the place was buzzing. The crowd outside was there for a large one, and I felt caught up in the expectation of it all in a way that I'd not sensed for years. This was like walking into Rock City; fired up and ready to give it all I had. The gig delivered and the buzz of standing on stage, getting dead excited as I MCed over the tunes, telling people to get their hands in the air, getting the whistle posse making some noise and all that confirmed that this was where I wanted to be. Andy, Dean and Carl were into it and from then on I was in.

Actually when I say in, it wasn't right to the heart of the outfit that I went. At the end of the day Bizarre Inc was those three guys. The rest of us, singers, dancers and myself, were all just part of the live show in those early days. When it came to getting creative in the studio it was all about Andy, Dean and Carl banging out the tunes. But none of that mattered really. I was having a laugh with them, turning up to the odd gig now and then, maybe working a night a week DJing in some club around Manchester, but all that really mattered was Shelly's. I had to be there every Saturday night, and if I wasn't then something was seriously wrong.

As ever, Shelly's was a popular place, and if I'd turned up too late it would mean taking second best over the road at the harder-edged Entropy. Not that this was all bad, and we had some top nights there. There was one time when I made a nuisance of myself with Mickey Finn while he was DJing. Someone shoved me in the booth with him and I found myself with a mic in my hand, rapping over some tune or other. He liked it and asked me if I wanted to rap on his forthcoming single. Being battered out of my head made deciding difficult; should I take a risk with Mickey Finn and hope that his big name pulled off or stay with the Bizarre Inc crew, who I liked a lot? I was only getting £100 per night that I was on stage with them, but there was something about them that secured my loyalty. It was odd too, as none of them took any gear. Apart from a bit of weed they steered well clear of the Class As. Knowing that they'd just sacked their previous MC for getting a little too high 'n' happy, I made sure I kept things to myself.

Money was a funny one. I never got the impression that any of them were in it for the cash. There seemed to be a bit of it around, not huge amounts but enough for Andy and the others not to be signing on, but it certainly wasn't the reason why they were together. Or at least that's what I thought until I met the manager, Anthony. He just seemed to me like one of their old mates from way back, the kind of guy who if it wasn't for them, he probably would have been blagging a living from mates down the pub. I didn't like him much, and I don't think he knew what he was doing. Yeah, he was dependable, but as for taking them where they wanted to be within the industry long term, his ideas ran out pretty quickly – not that long after a few top ten hits, as it turned out. Still, that wouldn't have been the first time I was mistaken. I remember Andy playing me their new single, 'I'm Gonna Get You', and I told him I thought it wasn't hard enough. To me it sounded like a flimsy little pop tune, but with MK remixing and plenty more hype backing it up I was proved spectacularly wrong. It was their biggest ever hit, eventually reaching number three in the national charts.

Originally they'd used a sample in the track and wanted me to mime for TV it when we came to do it live (or as near to live as we ever did things) I was called to do it for them. Didn't bother me either way, and miming at least meant that I had less work to do. In those early days it was best that I didn't have too much to worry about, as I was pretty much blown away by the appearances on *Top Of The Pops*. This was my first time to a TV studio and walking in there had me coming over all childish. I couldn't stop giggling every time I saw the show's logo printed and it was about all I could do to stop myself from nicking whatever memorabilia wasn't nailed down.

Having turned up at about 8 a.m., we had to do something like three dress rehearsals without any crowd in there so that they could get the cameras worked out. But that was it for the day, and by the time it came to the recording I was bored and in desperate need of some stimulation. Wizz, boredom and being stuck in a small room was never a recipe for a good mood, and when we finally got to do a take and they let the crowd in I was not best pleased. They all seemed to be about 12 years old and the whole thing sent me right down. All I could do was think of how much I hated 12-year-olds and wonder why I was doing this anyway, especially as I stood to earn no extra money out of the record sales. I got 125 quid off the TV producers for turning up, but that was about it. Somehow it didn't quite seem worth doing a turn as Bongo the Clown for the little 'uns.

'I'm Gonna Get You' went massive and it freaked me out. I'd be watching the telly and suddenly the tune would be there in the background as the football highlights played, or walking down the street and someone would be mumbling 'Yo DJ pump this party' to themselves. It was mad, but I couldn't take it too seriously; I knew my place and that was on the edge of the band. The three lads at the core were the real band, me, the singers and dancers were just a little extra window-dressing.

Still, we had to be ready to pull it out the bag if we had to. One day we were at a studio to mime a performance for a show called *The Beat* with Gary Crowley. Unfortunately someone had brought the wrong DAT and the only backing track we had was an old version of 'Playing With Knives' without any vocals on it. Angie had to sing the part live and I had to do the same with the rap.

The results weren't great and I think it reminded Andy, Dean and Carl just how important a part of the band's live success I was.

But I was having a laugh and Andy and I were getting on well. There were lots of parties, lots of meetings with famous people, lots of worrying that I might end up looking as rough as that bloke out of the Stereo MCs. As the single took off in the mainstream we started to play more Shaz and Trace clubs, and even though places like The Hippodrome were a bit of a laugh, there are only so many of them that you want to see. After all, it was this wet T-shirt way of doing things that I'd ODed on out in Spain. Getting back into it was not what I had in mind.

But New York, now that was more my thing. The single had taken off in America at the same time as the UK and we were straight off on a 30-date club tour across the country. I was loving it and even though I was only on 100 quid a day, the thought of coming back to three grand kept me sweeter than sweet.

The first stop was at the label, Columbia. I was busy giving the nod and the wink to anyone that looked my way, desperate to get some gear, but they weren't having any of it. Perhaps it was that which put me in a bad mood, but seeing all the Bizarre Inc posters around the foyer got me feeling all cynical. I was sure that as soon as we were out of there the posters would be ripped down and the next guests' smiling faces would be plastered all over the walls.

The hotel – the Chelsea (which I later found out was one of the more impressive rock 'n' roll hotels to be seen in) – was our home from home for the duration. I'd been getting myself so hyped up about the city, the limos and the rest of it that I'd managed to totally miss the action that was going on throughout the hotel. The foyer was rammed with teenagers (not for us, that's for sure) and there was a buzz running throughout the place that was difficult – but not impossible – to ignore.

I was sharing a room with Andy, and was staring out of the window when he came in, having returned from an interview downstairs.

'You know Take That?' he asked me. 'Well, they're staying here too. We must be doing something right.'

At the time they were big – certainly big over in the UK – but it was only just beginning for them in America. I guess that's why I was surprised that the hotel was so charged up with security personnel; it all seemed a bit over the top for a group that hadn't broken the US charts yet. While I was musing on their success it suddenly hit me that if Take That were here then Jason Orange would be here too. It had been a while since we'd seen each other – those Street Machine days were a long time ago now – but it would be nice to catch up with him. So I put a call in to reception asking to be transferred to his room. No chance. I left a message for him telling him what room I was in and concluded that was the end of the matter.

Dean and Carl came in and we started having a go at the mini-bar. We were chatting about the hotel and the meeting we'd all had at the record label earlier when there was another knock on the door. Carl opened it to reveal two of the largest bouncers I'd ever seen. I bottled it, convinced they were security guards come to take me away. I'd forgotten the fact that I had no drugs on me, but I bricked my load nevertheless. Things calmed down when out from behind them stepped Jason, Howard and little Mark.

We chatted for a while, then I played host and introduced my good friend Jason to the gawping Andy, Carl and Dean. Those were some serious points to score and I sat back and soaked it up as the six of them chatted about record labels, tours, management and all the things I had little knowledge of and absolutely no interest in.

Our first New York gig was that night in Heaven, a converted church with the kind of atmosphere that made you grin from ear to ear, no matter how straight you were. Luckily we didn't have to worry about that for long, as some bloke sorted us out with a bit of weed. It was good and strong, strong enough for me not to worry about having nothing else to go with it, but it was a different story for the band. They were battered and spent the whole gig standing absolutely still, staring into the crowd of hyped-up queens. After our 40 minutes were up we went off, and I was about to lay into them for doing a Pet Shop Boys on us when Andy stopped me.

'I never saw it before,' he mumbled, looking like someone had just switched a light on in his brain. 'I never knew what people saw in Bizarre Inc. But now ...' and he wandered off to feel surprised on his own. Poor bloke; he'd been making all this great drug music for so long and he'd never really experienced it himself.

When we got back to the hotel Andy got a bit more sociable and we ended up stoking up the old weed fire within us and sitting down to write some songs. We were dead excited and started calling ourselves the new Lennon and McCartney. It was the weed talking and the songs were your typical stoned ramblings:

> *She floats away on a butterfly's wings*
> *Reaching the light beyond her dreams*

The rest of the tour was pretty much the same; rammed full of gigs, drugs, hotels and a wide-eyed bunch of English lads who couldn't believe their luck. It's amazing what a couple of limo rides can do to you, and it didn't take long before we were feeling like regular stars, soaking up the hype and all that. But a tension set in and the band began to form into a couple of groups; Carl and Angie were together doing their own thing while Dean, Andy and I were sticking together for most of the time. I wasn't sure what was going on but something told me that Carl's days were numbered.

Sorted

The tour ended with a week spent in San Francisco. Apart from a run-in with some nasty drug called Ice the stay there was pretty uneventful, but the city made a massive impression on all of us. It was like some 60s throwback with acid casualties all around the place and an atmosphere that was totally relaxed. We all loved it and came back with wardrobes full of tie-dye and spangly threads. I reckon we thought we were the new, white Jackson Five or something, and when we returned it felt as if things were going to change for the band.

Just as we'd left the UK the third single, 'Took My Love', had been released. That was a bit of a cock-up, as to be without band-promotion for 30 days won't do any single many favours. As suddenly as the rush of feeling like a celebrity had come on, the frustrations set in too. It was all getting to be a bit much, and going straight from Heathrow to a studio to film an appearance in some kids' TV show was not my idea of fun. Twelve-year-olds have never been my ideal companions, and I began to make a habit of being rude to any one of them that asked for an auto-graph or whatever. What had started out as an underground act, playing Shelly's and the like, had suddenly become a pop thing and I wasn't sure I was all that bothered. Actually that's not true; I wasn't sure I was all that well paid. Money was the main thing on my mind, and as I was only on a daily rate I realized that not only was I probably not going to get rich out of it, but that it could disappear in an instant.

There was one final *Top Of The Pops* appearance though. 'Took My Love' made it onto the show by the skin of its teeth, and we were called up to do the honours. Now that I was a seasoned pop star, now that I'd 'done' America, now that I'd mingled with Take That in NYC, I left the wide-eyed Cam behind. There was no sense of occasion, or at least I didn't make an effort to be at the studios either on time or in any fit state to do my job. It was all part of the image.

ASCENSION

So I wasn't too happy when, sitting in the canteen, trying not to do too much that might make me feel any worse than I did right then, I looked up to see a baby in front of me. More than just a baby, it was Annie Lennox's baby – or at least one that she was borrowing for the day. Annie was chatting away, standing sideways on to me with the baby resting on her hip. The kid was staring at me, little globs of spit and mucus hanging out of its mouth. I couldn't cope with it, but I was trapped. Suddenly the fact that this Scottish singer in front of me was a household name bothered me. I needed to get out and go to the toilet, but pushing past her, inconveniencing her in any way, was a no-no in my strangely twisted mind. So I stayed where I was and puked into my lap. I'm sure Annie was impressed and certainly grateful that I'd not bothered her. As I sat there, cradling a lap full of thigh-warming vomit, she smiled at me and I suddenly felt even worse. Damn this rock 'n' roll lifestyle, I thought.

Not that puking is particularly symbolic, but it kind of sums up what happened for the band. We just sort of broke down, stopped working the way we were supposed to. The San Francisco vibe was still strong within them and the band went into the studio soon after coming back from America to record a new album. Instead of being full of rave anthems it took on a more funky flavour, and I reckon it was some of their best work. Still, I'm no label boss and the ones with the cheque books didn't rate the stuff. Things just never really got that big for them again.

Looking back now it's easier to see the wider picture, and during 1992 the whole dance culture underwent a massive change. While Bizarre Inc were taking the sounds of the underground up to the surface there was a massive influx of people to the clubs. Gradually dance music became the norm rather than rock or pop. When advertisers looked for a soundtrack they increasingly turned to the clubs for the tunes, and the same has to be said of fashion. High street shops moved towards a slightly more glam set of costumes, a welcome step on from the baggy knitwear phase that had threatened to engulf the whole of the UK throughout the early part of the 1990s.

And it wasn't just the shops that showed signs of taking an interest in the clubs. Hardcore clubbers found that more and more of their mates who had spent the previous few years wondering just exactly what it was they were into suddenly were taking an interest and tasting it for themselves. High street clubs began putting on midweek dance nights and lads had to get used to the idea of dancing. No more jackets and ties for the night out spent standing around the edge and pointing at women. Those early days when club and mainstream culture were introduced were funny times, like the most awkward of first dates. Some of the lads would still consider dancing to be something that laid their masculinity open to question and some of the ladies were still glued to their stilettos, which I guess is why handbag took off.

Anyway, the point is that this was a new market and people hungry for a little easy cash began to catch on to the idea that money could be made out of the ever-increasing popularity of clubbing. Embarrassing as it might be, I have to put my hands up and say that I was one of them. But it was a big wave we all were riding and I'm sure nothing could really have been done to hold back the commercialization of club culture. Still, that's not much consolation when it's so hard to find a club these days that doesn't have the dirty fingerprints of the money men all over it. Back in 1992 it was just a simple way of making money, and I was first approached by a bunch of people in Nottingham called Trapeze Productions to help out putting on some nights in Manchester.

I'd been working with a guy called Tim Howard, messing about in the studio and doing a few DJ sets wherever we could, and together we formed a plan; if we could get the 21 Piccadilly nightclub we'd be laughing. It was a classic meat market, the sort that hadn't been touched by a southerner for years. Short skirts and stilettos, broken glass and sticky floors. Perfect.

The deal was this: if Tim and I secured the club for one night a week for four weeks, if we got flyers printed and made sure there was a bit of Manchester in the club, Trapeze would take us on as partners, splitting the profits. Tim didn't have much money and I had even less, so we ended up doing most of the donkey work, but the prospect of taking a month to earn some serious cash was about as good as it gets. I had nothing to put in, but then again nothing much else to do and nothing to lose.

We got a Tuesday and a Wednesday night a couple of weeks apart, set the price at a fiver and called it The Dream. We had some big, heavy-handed lads from Nottingham up to work the doors and worked hard at getting the word out on the street. We broke our backs for a couple of weeks before the first night, flyering all the local clubs and that, but the prospect of filling the club with people made it all worthwhile. With Trapeze's money behind it we were able to spend big, calling on some half-decent DJs from London – Stu Allen and Tony Ross from Kaos – putting in a nice sound system, a few lasers and generally making the club feel like the real thing. OK, so it was hardly Ku or Amnesia, but for central Manchester it rivalled The Hacienda for four weeks so it wasn't that bad.

The club's capacity was just over 2,000 people and on the first night we only managed to pull in 400. Gutted. We'd made a loss, but still the bare bones of the night were wicked. We carried on with the next night, this time having Jumping Jack Frost, Grooverider from London and Nipper from Manchester as the main attractions. They paid off as the second time we got 1,000 people through the door. This was more like it. Again we made a loss, but not too heavy a one. We could taste the buzz in the crowd and knew that we were only a couple more nights away from filling the place out. We persuaded the club to let us have the Thursday slot, carried on into January of 1993, and by our fourth ever night we'd changed our name to Reality and had hit the magic 2,000 number.

Until then the manager of the club had been happy. OK, so we'd taken over his student night, but there'd been no trouble and the club was fuller than usual. But hitting capacity meant that people began to notice, and by the time we'd done five nights Salford turned up to see what was what. Things got heavy. Someone got glassed at the bar and one of the doormen got stabbed. Salford just couldn't let something big happen in Manchester without them being a part of it. The manager was livid and pulled the plug. It seemed like a bit of an over-reaction to me, but we later found out that he'd been sent some bullets in the post and had had it made clear to him that Salford were out for running his doors. Not a pleasant prospect for any person, and despite the fact that he'd been doing nicely out of it all he cancelled all our bookings in one afternoon. We were gutted, especially as I'd been making almost 1,500 quid each night we'd put the club on.

But it wasn't all Gunchester and gang violence. Salford were like some wild animal in that they only felt threatened by size. Our nights were a beacon that told them money was to be found there, but around that time there were plenty of other much smaller nights going off without their helpful assistance. One of my favourites was Luved Up's Reason To Be Gurning night. The venues were only ever 300 or 400 capacity and the two lads who ran them wanted nothing more than to provide a nice atmosphere for the smiling E-heads of the area. They gave people bags of sweets as they came in, covered the floor in balloons and scattered party poppers all over the place. They mixed in a little 70s disco with the pumping house and pulled in bongo and didgeridoo players to add a little of that Ibiza magic to the proceedings. They were great nights, not only because they encouraged everyone there to play and have fun but because they were safe. And safety counted for a lot in those days.

By 1993 Bizarre Inc had faded from my life. They were still doing bits here and there, but it was a different phase. I'd had my fun with them and had moved on. There were new things going on all around me, but as long as I was getting my pills and powder I was happy. It turned out that our time pretending to be promoters wasn't wasted at all, as I ended up being offered a slot at 21 Piccadilly at the weekends. It was a bit closer to Alicante than I wanted, but at least I came out on Sunday morning with a few hundred quid in my pocket. Of course the fact that I was working at the weekend meant that I was missing out on some of the action that was going on, so I found myself hunting for big nights out midweek. The Brickhouse did a good one on a Tuesday and there were others on Wednesday and Thursday. The all-dayers on Sunday were a treat too, and within a few weeks I'd settled down to a nice rhythm of nocturnal living.

Having money helped. Somehow I got into skiing; driving up to Scotland and turning up at Glen Shee. I'd got into it all through a friend called Gem. I'd got to know her through the regular nights at Luved Up and found in her a friend as keen on wizz and E as I was. As I've said before, I'd never been that much into drugs that took you down, maybe I'd had enough of that with the glue, and being with people who smoked a lot of dope just did my head in. In the strange, twisted drug logic of my mind it was far better that I was taking stimulants like E and speed; I was keeping myself fit and healthy with all that running around. It's mad to think I actually believed that stuff too, but then again, I guess we've all lost our way a bit over the years.

There was something about being sat up a mountain, spliff in hand, that aided contemplation. I began to feel like a spiritual being again, to connect with some of those moments I'd had back in Ibiza. It wasn't as if I was becoming a philosopher or anything, and most of the thoughts were along the lines of 'the world is so big and I am so small', but it did me good to get out, to slow down and breathe again. With so much time spent inside clubs getting pounded by the tunes, just to be surrounded by total silence was a massive deal. I loved it and in some way it felt like my healing, or at least the beginning of it.

At times my mind would turn to traditional religion. It had struck me that clubs had always been very spiritual environments, with all those people going through indescribable experiences together, and despite the fact that I'd not been in a church since mass when I was a nipper, I was sure that clubs had taken their place. But what was the point of it all? Was there really just one way up, just one true faith? It didn't make sense, but thinking about it was a nice enough way to spend an afternoon.

What is man? Is he just a monkey that got lucky? Is he a freak of nature, a twist of fate and circumstance that led him to develop further and faster than the others? Would I even be thinking like this if I was just one of those lucky monkeys? What about those Tibetan monks? Have they got the right idea, sat in contemplation, trying to make themselves better people? Could I make myself a better person? Have I been making myself a better person? Have all the highs and smiles really meant that much? Has it all been a fake? Pills and powder, that's where my highs have come from, but what about the natural high? Does it exist? Can I find it? Should I have another spliff before I make my way back down the slopes?

WIZZ

ith Gem and me it was all about getting high. She was gay, Scottish and keen to take as many drugs as possible. A perfect combination for lots of laughs. She came from a town called Annan on the borders in Dumfriesshire. There never seemed to be much going on there, but as it was on the way up to Glen Shee we'd occasionally stop by and call in on her mum. It was fun helping Gem play the model daughter and even more amusing hearing her spin her mum some line about just what it was she was getting up to down there in Manchester. Her mum was a great lady and like so many of my mates, Gem wanted to protect her from the worry. E was beginning to make the news and even though this was before Leah Betts died, clubbers were already being portrayed as wild zombie maniacs intent on dragging inno- cent teenagers down into the pit of hell. These were the days of drug 'pushers' and the common idea that E was getting forced on unsuspecting kids. Of course the clubs told a different story; in there it was a seller's market, with the guys in puffa jackets deciding quality and price. We were queuing up to get to them, not the other way around.

Wizz

It was one day in April 1994 when we'd just completed the epic journey up to Scotland in my battered old Metro. It might not have been taxed or insured, or have had an MOT come to think of it, but it was perfect for gear. It had one of those perfectly flat bits of dashboard above the glove box and on it Gem and I would lay out all our drugs for the trip. She'd roll a few spliffs as we were leaving Manchester, and by the time we'd got out of the urban sprawl she had set up a few lines as well. She'd have to take the wheel while I pulled my seat forward and leant over to take them on board. From then on in the car was full of our mindless conversation as the whole journey filled with opinions on anything from girls to clubs to drugs to clothes to girls to clubs to drugs to clothes.

Having arrived in Annan after three hours on the road and a lot of excited conversation, and after Gem and I had been to call in at her mum's, we went over to meet one of her friends in the village. We drove away from the houses and after a while of driving through countryside I started to get confused.

'I thought she lived in the same village as your mam?'

'She does,' said Gem, 'and we've been driving on her land for ages.'

It didn't make much sense to my addled brain, but as we turned the corner a view opened up that had me wide-eyed and amazed. It was a huge house, the type of mansion that you see in a film. I waited in the car while Gem went in and came back out with this mad-looking goth. She introduced herself as Tori and we made our way back down the driveway to the local hotel for a few beers.

People always fell into one of two categories with me when I first met them: did they do gear or not? Tori looked like she did but there was only one way of telling, so I invited her into the toilets and gave her a line of wizz. We chatted fine after that. That was about it really. Gem and I had been telling her mate about what the clubs were like in Manchester and she sounded keen to come down. Suited me fine as, despite the fact that she was on a seriously weird fashion tip, I liked what I saw.

Tori was a funny one. She passed the gear test with flying colours, and she earned herself an extra credit by letting me know that she was up for finding out about any other mood-altering substances I could get my hands on. Result. But there was something else too: she was her own person. You know what it's like with clubs; the scene has such a strong identity, there is such a clear way of dressing, talking, behaving and dancing, that too often it can seem like new people you meet are all just a bit too fake, as if their whole identity has been constructed in the lab/bedroom before coming out. But Tori, well, she was different. She was more than a goth, and she eventually became far more than just a clubber. In a world where image and stuff are so important, she has remained unique. She does my soul good, giving me something to chase after myself.

A couple of weeks later and Tori came down to Manchester for a weekend. I'd been hoping that she was going to make it, but to be honest my mind had been taken up with a new toy. Gem had just started to introduce me to Manchester's gay scene, going along to Cruise and clubs like that. I suppose I was a bit unsure at first; my background hadn't exactly brought me into a lot of contact with that scene. But if ever I was beginning to wonder about the direction mainstream clubbing was taking, as soon as I was through the doors of somewhere like Cruise I knew I'd found that pure, decent buzz again. It was like going back to the mad nights at The Hacienda, when I'd walk away going 'I can't believe this is happening in my home town.' The gay scene had so much more to offer; an energy, flamboyance and extravagance that added so much to the music. Suddenly clubbing was fun again, and I was a happy lad.

So Tori came down and we all went out. On the way to Cruise Tori was giving me her opinion on Bizarre Inc. According to her they were one of the most annoying bands that had ever existed. It suited me fine; I liked gobby women. I wasn't so sure her taste was much better though, as she was a fully signed up Cure and Cult fan. Still, she was on my patch now.

It ended up fine. She told me she was straight, which answered one of my main questions about her, and I told her likewise. It was just a one-night stand; she didn't seem too keen on coming down to Manchester and I found out that she had two jobs, one working for a recovery company during the day and another driving HGVs at night. This was another reason for me not thinking much of it: I mean, a trucking goth? It wasn't quite my scene. She invited me to a truck fair and I was even more unsure.

But six months passed and Tori was down in Manchester every weekend. We had got together despite some serious barriers being in the way. I'm not talking about the clothes, the music or the trucks, but the fact that there always seemed to be a cloud hanging over her. A month or so in and I found out what. We were playing one of those 'Tell me a secret' games when Tori told me that she had been sexually abused by her father. I was so angry. I wanted to pay for the boys to go round to his house and sort him out. But there was a police investigation under way, one that was enquiring into what he had done to Tori over 10 years, to both her sisters, her aunty and her cousin. He was a wealthy businessman, one with connections and all that, the sort that felt he had the power to get things his own way. He came from money, and as Tori was constantly reminded by shocked relatives, people like them didn't do things like that. But he had done it and the police were on the case.

Tori and I were on the same mission. We were both out to get as high as possible as often as possible. It didn't matter where the party was, we'd be there, doing it large and making as much of an entrance as possible. Being one of those weird-dressing types, Tori took off in the gay scene and was soon delving into the realms of fetish wear and all that. Me, well, I'd always dressed to sweat and not much else, but for Tori going out meant dressing up. For a time we'd drive over to Vague in Leeds with her in thigh-high leather boots, rubber skirt, chains, gloves, SM cap and bra top, me following on behind feeling confused and excited all in one. The fact that it was all black made the transition easier for her, but soon she was wearing nothing but white: stockings, suspenders, Y-fronts, basque, hair in rags and a long flowing gown over the top. Somehow baggies didn't seem quite so crazy any more. But that all changed when I got my leather chaps, and then I was causing my own ripples of attention when we went out. It was all a bit of fun and worked well, as Tori wanted to attract the attention while I liked to revel in it.

Our lives were like a two-dimensional picture; in the background was the constant grief of the first police investigation into the abuse, but up on the surface was a manic few years spent immersing ourselves in club culture. It was classic escapism, and it did us good. Having got so close to Tori so quickly I was caught up in the emotion of the whole thing. Our party life became our way of coping.

Tori eventually moved down from Scotland officially, even though the first six months of our relationship were spent with her driving down each weekend and most midweeks too. The work at 21 Piccadilly had dried up and I was once again in the position of needing work. If I thought 21 was bad, taking me back down the path of the Alicante tack, I got a shock when I ended up working in Blackpool. I was desperate for cash and The Flagship was the only place I could get work as a DJ. It was scum through and through. It catered for people who were out to get as bladdered as possible for as little money as they could get away with. It was a pound-a-pint place with a massive turnover of people; they'd come in for 20 minutes, have a few beers and then be off out the door, on to another pub. I was up there in the DJ booth to keep the atmosphere frantic and to try and get the punters to stay for as long as possible. This was crowd manipulation using any means possible, and while I'd learnt a bit about using the tunes to mould the mood in a club, this kind of venue needed a less subtle approach. It was Alicante all over again; less mixing and more talking. I wasn't happy there, but walking away from two nights' work with not quite 400 quid was about the best I could hope for.

Tori got a job in the bar and we got to know Ian, the bar manager. He was as camp as a row of tents and would bitch like anything, but we both liked him straight away. He was off his face on E, Tori was tripping merrily along and I was on the wizz and whisky. We were a right threesome and were trying hard to develop the blags to make the evenings bearable. There were cameras behind the bars to make sure that the staff weren't drinking the profits away, but the cameras revolved and you had a decent window of opportunity every few minutes. I'd be stuck up in the booth all night and had to ask for my drinks over the PA, so I'd shout 'Mine's a large one' for a pint and 'Mine's a small one' for a whisky. It all worked fine in theory with us all covering each other's backs, but whenever Tori and Ian were too far gone I'd end up shouting 'Mine's a small one' over and over again. That never went down too well with the punters.

Ian carried on the good work Gem had been doing on us, introducing a whole new range of clubs that we'd never been in. First up were Funny Girls, a bar in Blackpool that was full of trannies and sex changers, as well as The Duncan, an after-hours place that was one of the strangest. It was a converted B&B with a bar downstairs populated by blokes looking like the biker out of The Village People. Upstairs was a different story, but we didn't spend much time up there. Ian was a good lad and introduced us to loads of people, and was always ready to jump in should things get a little heavy and heterophobic. But that hardly ever happened, and in general I've never felt so accepted by a group of people as I have by the gay community. It probably helped that neither Tori nor I dressed like your typical straight couple, but it worked on a deeper level. We were fully signed up to those core values, and our hearts were beating pretty much in time with theirs. OK, so we were straight, but as far as the dressing up, the hedonism, the excess and the pure sexiness of the scene went, we were like the rest.

Mantos, New York, Le Cage and The Paradise Factory, these were the backdrop to our evenings spent back in Manchester. Ian would come and stay in the flat I'd got and we'd all go out and have a mad one. The highs were massive with Ian, but the lows went down just as far. They were OK when the rest of us were up, but when all our lows coincided we were not a happy bunch to be around. Either silence would blanket us all in or we'd be at each other's throats. That makes me sad looking back on it, that we let the drugs say some things to each other that we didn't mean, but I guess that's just part of the price you pay. It's simple physics, isn't it: what comes up must come down.

Still, we made sure that the downs were as brief as possible. I never went back on the glue – there was too much of a stigma attached to it – but I'd have a free buzz with a trip if I had to. Tori was well into acid and used to buy a sheet of 100 at a time. She and Ian would knock out 30 or so at four quid each, mainly selling them to the other staff at The Flagship, make a few quid and keep back 20 for themselves. But for me acid was only there to be used as a last resort. It messed me up far too much and while I'd have a few giggles on the way up, I always seemed to end up more confused and bewildered than Tori or Ian. They just laughed the whole trip through, but hours would go by and I'd be trying to work out if I really was myself or a Russian spy playing myself as part of a plot to sabotage Britain's nuclear defence programme.

Things started to go wrong in January. Tori and I had been back up to Glen Shee to do a bit of skiing, having left Ian in the flat. We got back to find out that we'd all lost our jobs at The Flagship. We were gutted. The only option was to sign on. I'd never done it before, and even though I'd been in worse financial trouble before and always managed to get out of it somehow, this time I just didn't have the energy to let my pride get in the way. We managed at least to sort it so that we signed on different weeks. That way we always had some money for the basics. Pretty quickly the one-bedroom flat became the scene of some serious Young Ones living. Tori and I were in the bedroom while Ian was kipping on the couch in the main room. It wasn't much of a couch either: we'd nicked it from a club and it not only stank but it was the least comfortable couch ever made. We were skint, wasted, uncomfortable, overcrowded, low and heading even lower.

We'd shop in Netto or Aldi, buying bulk quantities of lentils and sausages. Spending money on food was a waste, but we knew that we needed at least a little sustenance each day. We always tried to make sure that we had enough money left over for drugs to go out on most nights, but on those rare occasions that we were stuck in we could only make it bearable by working our way through bottles of sherry and vermouth. At least I could still get into 21s without paying, and sometimes the bar staff would sort us out with some free drinks, but in general the first few months of '95 were not exactly high points.

I was looking for work but there didn't seem to be anything going. In the background there was something going on inside me, a change that was working its way out that somehow made the lifestyle seem slightly less than ideal. I don't know whether it was the stuff with Tori's dad or the comedown after the highs of Bizarre Inc, but as the days passed I began to feel less bothered about stuff. The midweeks became drawn-out hangovers with me coming down off the booze and wizz, Tori off her acid and Ian off his Es. We'd sit around, often in silence, waiting for the feelings to lift, waiting to feel better and get some motivation for doing something other than sit about waiting to feel motivated again. I could still get high, but it was getting harder to get out of it, to lose the plot and forget everything about anything. It was like trying to run underwater; your body moved as you wanted it to but at nowhere like the speed. I couldn't seem to shake off the heaviness and for the first time ever I began to wonder about whether there was more to life than all this.

Ian's lows were the worst out of all of us. Part of this was the drugs, part was just the way things were for him, but standing on the sideline and watching the way the scene worked it was hard not to feel hurt along with him from time to time. I know I've been shallow in my time, but some of the relationships in the gay scene would end for the strangest of reasons; someone thinner or with a better body would come along and you'd be chucked. Even someone new to the area could upset the balance and set off a chain reaction of break-ups and pain. I don't think it made him happy, and living with the threat of being dumped as soon as someone 'better' came along would be enough to mess with anyone's head.

Anyway, loads of times he'd go out at night and we'd expect to see him the next day. Instead we'd not see him for days. Liverpool, Macclesfield, Lancaster, you name it, Ian would phone up from there after a period of silence, not having a clue how he got there or how he was getting back. One Sunday afternoon we were all sitting around the flat feeling bored and that, when he told us he was heading down the town to see if he could get a couple of drinks out of someone. I was a bit worried as I'd got him an interview for a job as barman at 21s at 10 a.m. the next day. With Ian you never knew, so I think I probably went on about it a bit much as he was making his way out of the door, telling him not to end up skint and in Stoke or something like that.

A few hours later he phones up in a complete state. He was gibbering on about me phoning up 21s and cancelling the interview, about how sorry he was that he'd messed up and that.

'I don't know what happened but I must have fallen asleep and I'm sorry but it's 10.30 and the interview was half an hour ago and I'm sorry and it's just ...'

'Ian. Look around you. It's dark. It's Sunday night still.'

'Oh.'

Poor guy. He was often quite confused but he became like our little brother and we both loved him for it. He was rubbish at taking care of himself, but I was only marginally better. We'd get up at about 2 p.m. and spend the rest of the afternoon trying to work out what we were going to do that evening. Preparation was the key, firstly because having no money meant we had to be careful about what we did spend and how, and secondly because we had so much time on our hands we just had to fill it with something. So we'd get up and eventually a plan would form giving us some idea about where we were going to go, who we were going to meet and where we were going to end up. We wouldn't go out until about 10 at night, but I'd always have kept back a bit of wizz to help while away the afternoon. I had to be a bit sly with it though, as the others would have wanted a share. I'd disappear into the bathroom for an hour or so, have a line and try to get myself up and in the mood as soon as possible.

Evenings started with the usual trip round to the dealers. Kippo was an unusual type in that he had a supermarket approach to the whole thing. If you bought three you got a fourth free, so we'd always pool our fivers and get the extra. Somehow I managed to blag the fourth too, so by the time we moved on to a pub I'd be getting along quite nicely. Tori never drank, she didn't see the point of taking something that brought you down when you wanted to get up, but for me the booze just helped me get even more out of it. That's what I liked, losing the plot, feeling out of control, and the more spices I added into the pot the closer I could get to having my head blown off. We'd end up blagging into some club if we could, but the days of the flamboyant entrances and wild excess seemed to be fading. We just didn't have the cash or the heart for it.

Eventually Ian left and made his way down to Brighton. He came from a PR background and he managed to get himself a job with a firm down there. But booze and pills got in the way and before long he'd lost the job and was surviving by selling Es and working for a couple of trannies on the side. They'd pay him a tenner a night to go round putting their cards in the phone boxes and taking out the ones of the competition.

A few months later he was back. He'd hit rock bottom and the old crew were back together again. Somehow an old contact from the days of Trapeze Productions had got us both jobs at MGMs in Nottingham. I was DJing Friday and Saturday and Tori was dancing. It was the same old story though; the club was rough and my heart wasn't exactly in it. The money made it bearable but it all felt so tacky, a million miles away from the mad rush of Ku, Shelly's, Cruise and the others. Maybe I was getting old, but if you caught me at the right moment I'd bang on for hours about how things were so much better back in the days of 1990. And you know what? They were.

We were still living in the flat in Burnside Court. With the job in Nottingham at least it meant that we had some money, but the vibe was still the same. Life was a predictable ride of highs and lows and it felt as though we were all trying to keep ourselves away from that crushing sense of numbness that sets in when the drugs wear off. Looking back on it now I'm not even sure why it was that we all ended up this way, but it's probably all due to a cocktail of different influences. The poverty, the lack of hope the pain of Tori's past and the tensions of living together in such a small space. I don't know. It just didn't seem like fun any more, and we all felt the same.

But hey, there was always someone calling up for a mad one and these moments of introspection never seemed to last too long. Just a call and a shout of 'doyouwannacomeoutandgethigh' was enough to make the cloud lift a bit and the dissatisfied thoughts move over and allow the good vibes of the moment to stand at the front of the class. Still, there was something about those evenings that we'd seen before. It was Tori who started to get bored first – I suppose I was more used to it, so close that I never really questioned it – pointing out that six hours of conversation that followed the same pattern might not be the ideal way of spending every night:

'TUNE!' someone would say whenever the DJ pulled out a good one.

'Youarright?' someone else would ask.

'Me? Off my face. You?'

'Onnarush.'

And that was it. Not that we were turning our backs on the whole scene, but doing it every night without the resources to get truly high or the energy to make it different meant that things were getting stale. Like I said, I'm not sure that the reasons lie in one single influence, I reckon it was more a cocktail of the whole lot of them that caused the frustrations to set in. We'd all talk a lot more when we were coming down, but again it was always about the drugs; what we saw, what we felt, what plot we nearly lost or what aches and pains we had the day before.

I suppose it all tied in with my death wish. Ever since I can remember I've been convinced that I'd not live beyond the age of 30. I'm glad that I've proved myself wrong on that score, but almost until the day itself, I never thought I'd make it to my 30th birthday. I'm not sure where it came from, and I don't remember being a big

Jimmy Dean fan as a nipper. There's something about it that matches up to the old teenage view that says 'I'm so hard that I'm going to kill myself', but it was deeper than that, becoming almost like a superstition. By this time in 1995 I was getting on for 27 years old and failing to live beyond the next three years just seemed like a fact. It infected all other parts of me, so I guess it's hardly surprising that I found it hard to feel good about things.

For most of my life I'd never paid much thought to death itself, always seeing it as the ending that capped off the mother of all parties. It was vague and too far away to contemplate fully, but as the old clock began to tick away my thoughts changed. I started to wonder what death was like. Would it hurt? What would it feel like? Where would I go? I'd worked out that we all had a spiritual side, but to me that spirituality belonged on this side of death. As far as what came after it, I just thought it was a short pain followed by a long rest. Enter into whatever spiritual realm you can on this side and don't worry about the rest. To me, and so many others who've popped pills and powder and ended up feeling as though they've discovered some kind of truth, everything was internal. Getting high was a case of cause and effect; if I took this I felt like that. Simple. The same applied for matters spiritual; if I believed in that my life after death would look like that. Take your pick.

Part of the credit has to lie at the feet of ketamine. It's famous for producing those out-of-body experiences, ones where you feel as though you can float away and look back on yourself. Snorting it was a bad idea but I did it all the same. It wasn't exactly fun, but it made me think about stuff, and when I did it back in 1993 it seemed to change things for me. I reckon that was where most of my thoughts about death and spirituality and whatever else all started. I was a right laugh.

I suppose everyone comes to a point where they start to look around for some kind of deeper meaning to their lives. After all, you've got to be pretty brave to be happy believing that we are here for no real reason other than our parents having sex and that our future consists of death and nothing else. To answer the question 'What's the point of life?' with 'There is no point' never appealed to me. Perhaps if I'd been stronger I could have coped with it, but somehow I've always wanted to know that there was some reason, some point to it all. If feeling high comes from taking on board certain chemicals I wanted to know what was the force that kicked us into being.

By the time that summer came around I was ready to get stuck into some serious question-and-answer sessions. I looked back over my life and wondered what had gone on and why and how. It seemed that I'd always been a bit on the shallow side, you know the sort of thing; following the crowd, wanting to impress, playing to an audience and all that. Nothing wrong with confidence and that in itself as it's a natural part of my personality, but putting too much store by how people feel about me, well, that always seemed to lead me into trouble.

To me club life had changed. It had gone from a group thing, an activity that was marked by a sense of community and unity, and become an individual activity. Standing in the middle of Space or Ku, surrounded by Spaniards, Italians, Dutch, Germans and Brits, it always blew my mind that the music was uniting us. We were part of something bigger than each of us and it felt great. Standing in the booth at 21s felt different; clubbing had become about the individuals much more than the collective. Perhaps it was all tied in with the scene becoming far more universal and mainstream, and I guess it's hard to feel united when there are so many people doing it all over the place. Back in the days of the underground, it was a real surprise to meet someone who took gear and stuff and if you caught up with friends you hadn't seen for years you'd be keen to find out if they were or weren't in the club.

But it had all changed, and the questions about the scene formed the backdrop to a whole load more questions about everything else that was going on in my life. I think everyone at some point stops and looks for a deeper meaning to life. This was my time to do it and I spent the summer of 1995 turning over loads of thoughts about the point of it all. I think I wanted to know that life was about more than just the experiences I'd been having. Mad as they were, there had to be more. I also reckon that we all need change, that shifting direction is as inevitable a course on the menu of life as pain, happiness, birth and death. Whether it's the scenery or an entire outlook, change must come and we must go with it. For some this happens with relationships, that getting married or breaking up brings in the necessary, but for others it might be getting into religion or changing location. I'd had enough of moving about and as far as relationships went me and Tori were just fine as we were, so I started to look to the spiritual side of things.

Tori and I were over at my brother's house one day early on in that summer and thankfully things had got better between him, his wife and myself. We all got on well, much better than when I was sponging off them earlier on, and I was busy asking them about religion. Now neither of them were exactly what you would call religious types, but Trish had been interested enough in it all when she was younger. She had a few books on the whole range of stuff, mainly leaning towards a New Age tip. There wasn't much conversation to be had on the matter but she was happy enough to lend me a copy of a book she had on world religions.

For the next few weeks the book became my trade catalogue and I'd flick through it, checking out the key points on offer. Buddhism did a nice line in peace and tranquillity, while Islam offered a discipline and sense of community that had been missing from my life for far too long. I'd chew each one over, picturing myself doing the stuff like I could see in the pictures.

Wizz

My affections wandered over each of them and my preferences would vary from one day to the next. Ian had got into Buddhism too, and even though he had moved out into his own flat on the Odsall Road, we still spent loads of time together. It hadn't stopped him having a good time, which counted for a lot in my book, but I also thought that he was more into it from the fashion perspective than anything much deeper. He was a Prada Buddhist and I don't think it lasted that long.

Out of the blue a couple of things happened. The first thing was *The Doors*, Oliver Stone's movie. It had been out for years but Tori and I suddenly got into it. We'd trip and watch it over and over again and the idea of plugging into a greater consciousness, of taking some serious drugs on board and getting in touch with whatever wise man was drifting through the ether at the time, appealed big time. Not only did it seem easy, but it kept the old drug intake nice and high and didn't lay down any of those rules. I suppose I'd tasted a few of those trippily spiritual highs in my time and thought that with a little more work and concentration, I too could break on through to the other side, ride the snake and do whatever else it was that Jim Morrison did.

The second and more important thing that came out of the blue was some work. I'd kept up with Tim Howard, an old mate from the days of The Dream and Reality, and while I'd slipped back into a bog of tacky clubs and bombed-out lethargy, he'd been working hard at things, making music and all that. He had a plan, and more than that, he had a manager. A bloke called Stevo was lined up, and his CV wasn't that bad at all. He'd managed Soft Cell and groups like that and happened to be dating Cleo Rocos, the busty young wench from the days of *The Kenny Everett Television Show*. Cleo hadn't done much since Kenny had hung up his giant hands and punk outfits, and wanted to get back into the limelight. So Tim, Cleo and I were brought together.

163

Now I wouldn't exactly call Vertigo a supergroup, but together we had a bit of talent. Cleo guaranteed some tabloid exposure, Tim worked hard and produced some wicked tunes and I – well, let's just say I was there to keep the others company. I might have been a bit down at the time, but I could still get myself up when the need arose.

This all happened in the June of 1995. We went straight into the studio within a week of getting together and put down a track called 'Beneath The Sheets'. It was a sexy little number, mainly because Cleo wasn't exactly Martha Wash, so we got her to sexily breathe the words out, whispering them along to the beat. As I remember, Pete Tong got into it a bit, it got to number three in the dance charts, but nothing else happened. Still, it wasn't a total failure and Stevo was up for putting a couple of grand more into it to see if we couldn't record a follow-up single.

We were booked into a studio in Manchester, a small one just outside the centre. The engineer there was all right, a laid-back guy named Zarc who played things a little differently from most other engineers I'd worked with. The normal thing to expect was to see them start the session off by rolling a big spliff, and get increasingly stoned as the hours passed by. I wasn't that much of a perfectionist or a professional that I minded, but I did notice that bright-eyed Zarc seemed to care about the music. He was interested in the sounds and all that, and I thought I'd talk things over with him. I was looking for lyrics and had taken my world religions book into the studio with me, telling him that I was looking for inspiration that might help with lyrics. I wanted the music to capture some of the things I was looking for myself and hoped that the book would help.

I don't know how I did but I knew that Zarc was a Christian. To be honest he was a bit of a stereotypical Christian; you know, a bit stiff and all that. But he was a nice guy and never rammed what he believed down my throat. He wasn't much help with the lyrics, but it seemed to spark some kind of conversation that ran over the days we spent recording. At the end of it all I was flying high, happy to have got the job done and have another single under my belt, I suppose I was high on the expectation that this might be it, the big break to help me and Tori out of the constant cycle of half-highs and frustration. I bought Zarc a bottle of champagne and wrote on the tag 'To Zarc, thanks for all your spiritual encouragement'. I don't know why I did it, but it just seemed like a nice thing to write at the time. His mate Andy was in the corner, Bible tucked under his arm. When he saw what was written on the card he piped up:

'We should save it until you become a Christian, Cameron.'
Yeah! Right.

Zarc and I had got on well, and he'd invited me to his wedding. I went along to it the next week and was amazed by what I saw. It was in a church but the location was about where the similarities stopped. I'd been used to bells and smells, rules and all that, but his service had drums and guitars and that in it. I told him afterwards that I reckoned they'd moved things on a bit since I was last inside one of them buildings.

But that was it as far as I was concerned. The single was over and the future of Vertigo depended on how well it did. Being honest with myself, I wasn't sure that anything would come of it. After all, Bizarre Inc had been fun and that, and I'd got closer to success than I'd thought possible, but it had all vanished in an instant. We put so much emphasis on getting those chart placings, but there are thousands of people out there like me who've been part of a band that's tasted a little bit of success only to find that life comes back down to earth pretty soon after. We had our four top ten hits, the three lads had made a bit of money, but as far as anyone else was concerned the group became yesterday's news the minute London Records lost interest. It's a fickle game and there are no guarantees.

ASCENSION

And so the summer of '95 took on a new twist: realism. I'd been searching for answers for a few months, but it was time to face up to the reality of the life of Cameron Dante. I'd had a laugh, enjoyed some highs along the way, but it was time to stop the bullshit. I'd been getting high since before I was a teenager, and now at the age of 27 I was tired. In Tori I'd found my soul mate, someone who I didn't have to try to impress, someone I could sit down with and be the real me. The way I saw it, we'd come from massively different backgrounds but something had clicked. We'd both spent our first nine months together getting off our faces and having a mad one, but somehow after that it all changed. The highs weren't so great and the lows weren't so easy to shake off. But in the middle there was something else that came through; a happiness of being together. Happiness ... contentment ... words I hadn't used for years. To me the good times were described by words like high, rush and hedonism, but with Tori they came in other ways too; the security of knowing that someone cares, the satisfaction of knowing that someone understands, the safety of knowing that not every good moment is naturally followed by a comedown. With Tori the laws of physics went out the window. With her another possibility came into the mix: could there be something more lasting? Was there a contentment that never faded, a happiness that refused to fade?

We didn't know where we were going to find it but it made sense that if it was going to come our way we ought to be straight. So we went along to Boots and bought ourselves the DIY detox kit. For three days we took no drugs, drank no coffee or tea, ate no fatty foods and drank this concentrated liquid dissolved in water. We flushed it all out of our system, and the three days were the strangest I can remember. I'd not been straight for years and not a day had gone by since I was an early teenager that I hadn't shoved something in my body to alter my mood. At the least it was booze and fags and at the other extreme it was, well, whatever was going. But enough was enough; I'd spent too long with these outside influences dictating how I felt and who I was. Now it was time to find the real me.

The questions filled my mind. Was this really the right way to go about finding the real me? What would I do once I had found him? What if I didn't like him? What if he didn't like me? What came next? This was a fresh page, a new start, but I felt shaky, totally unsure about where I'd end up. This physical detox was the final stage; I think I'd gone through the withdrawals of all sorts of other influences over the previous few months. The frustrations with the club scene had begun to get the tack out of my system and the quest for meaning through my world religions book was my way of kicking the old 'me first' lifestyle into touch. The 'dead by 30' was out too; I'd been searching for meaning but also trying to take control of my own life. I wasn't stupid and I knew that if I carried on taking whatever I was taking then my body might not go the distance. It wasn't on the verge of packing up as I entered decade number four, but I could hardly see myself managing to hang on until I was into the custard cream phase of 80something retirement homes.

No. This was me now, facing a new dawn. A fresh start. A new beat. I didn't have a clue what was going to come next, but as long as something did, well, that was just about fine with me. I'd spent a fair bit of time as a DJ over the years controlling the party vibe, and I'd rapped the old 'yo DJ pump this party' line with Bizarre Inc. Now it was time to really take control, to pump the party just the way I wanted it.

So I'm standing here at 9.07 p.m. When I was at Zarc's wedding last week he got one of his mates to give me a flyer for some gig he was involved in. It was only seven days ago but it seems like seven years. I remember saying that church had moved on a bit since I'd last been there. He smiled. Told me to come along to something new. What did he call it? 'Church as you've never seen it.' I've had the flyer in my pocket ever since. I must have read it 20 times every day since and I know the words off by heart. Don't know why; it's not exactly much of a flyer. 'Planet Life,' it says, 'Saturday 16th September, 8pm @ St Mary's Parish Church, Cheadle.' Can't say I've ever heard of Cheadle making much of an impression on the club scene, let alone a venue called St Mary's. But I'm here anyway, in the car park outside St Mary's. I can hear a 4/4 thud coming from inside the building, but not much else. Something about it has had me feeling nervous all week, as if it's something I've really got to go to. And that's it exactly; since I got the piece of paper shoved into my hand I've never thought that I wouldn't go. Tori told me not to bother, that it was the worst choice in all that world religions book. I think I agree too; Christianity hardly gets much of a write-up. All the rules of Islam with none of the community. It seems like constant misery, a ticket to feeling like you're worthless and scum. But if that's the story on paper, in the flesh it seems different. Or at least in Zarc's flesh it seems different.

I've always lived my life by feelings. Mostly it's been the ones on the up that have caught my eye, but this one is different. I'm nervous. I've got nothing inside me that's helping me move either way. I've been stood here 45 minutes, my stomach in knots but my heart feeling light. My stomach has told me to go home, my heart's been telling me to go in, but I've just stood here smoking. Why do I feel like a 14-year-old all over again? This feels like walking up the stairs with Amanda Jenkins, only much worse. Smoke another fag. Last one.

I need to be careful here. I know that the last few days have been odd, what with being on that detox thing and all. That finished yesterday and I've gone back on the ciggies already, but nothing else though. They taste too good to give up. A good long draw on them and the nicotine calms me right down. What was I saying? Oh yeah, I need to be careful. My head's in bits. I mean, it's not used to feeling like this; clean and light, without any other influences bashing around. I feel like my eyes are open, as if they've been half shut for years. It's like being up that mountain in Glen Shee, all freshness and quiet. I like it. Maybe whatever happens I'll stay straight after this. No more wizz or Class As at least.

The cigarette's finished. It's 9.16. I'm going in. I've never felt less spiritual than this. I've never felt so much apart from something larger than me. Do I feel alone? Is that why I'm here? Am I one of those weak people that need church as a crutch? What am I saying? What am I doing even thinking about this sort of stuff? Am I going to make some kind of decision tonight? I'm just going along to Zarc's gig though, what could be less important than that?

Enough. I'm going in.

They're all singing. Arms in the air, pumping 4/4 beat and 500 people crammed into some kind of old, old church, so old that it feels like it's been here since the dawn of time. It's like Glen Shee; big and old, natural, solid. But it's loud too. The sound system's cranked up and the lights are like the old ones we used to hire for The Dream and Reality three years back. I used to get such a rush of those strobes, especially with all that smoke rising up. But I'm not rushing now, at least not in the way I usually do. Or am I? Is that a little tingle down my spine? Take a deep, long breath, Cam, sort your head out.

That must have been the last song as some bloke's up on stage now calming everyone down, making us sit down. It's like being back at school, this. I haven't been sat down, facing the front as someone gives a lesson for years. I never liked them much then, but now it's better. He's talking about how everyone has a longing inside of them. Everyone has something that needs to be satisfied. That longing can't go without food for long.

'People fill the hole inside of them with sex, money, drugs.' How does he know? It's me. It's me. I've done that. That's what all this has been about – the last few months of getting dissatisfied with the drugs, of searching for some kind of meaning in life. That's why. It makes sense. What he's saying sums me up; looking for fulfilment, looking for something to satisfy.

And here comes the bit I know is on the way. I know before he says each word what it's going to be: you need God. I knew it. I knew it. I knew what he was going to say. I knew that was it. I knew it.

Do I?

I'm not rushing now. It all feels cold and quiet. I feel calm. I feel clean. He wants people to stand up. He's telling people that if they want this stuff they've got to stand up. Do I? Do I need God? Can I make it on my own? Of course I can – I have this far. Haven't I? But do I want to keep going now I know what I'm lacking? I don't know what this is about. I don't know what this all has to offer me. I don't know what is going on. But the longing, yeah, that's it, the longing that he was just talking about. That's me. That's Cameron summed up in a word: longing. I've been after it for years, never knowing what it really looks like. If there is a God, then he can show me. Yeah, that's it, a deal. If he's there, let him show me. Do I need him? Yes. I do. I want Jesus. I'm standing up.

THE GAP

That was five months ago. What a night. Things changed after that, and since then it's all been different. But you know what? it's been kind of the same too. This is no 'My Glorious Life' story I'm trying to sell you; it's just meant to be told the way it is. Things changed for me. I changed. I'm still here.

Vertigo changed. Surprisingly my pop career has not undergone a phoenix-like rising from the ashes of obscurity. Even Cleo's assets weren't enough to get us the exposure we needed, and 'Beneath The Sheets' never made it further than the manager's tape drawer. Surprised? Don't be stupid.

The first real turnaround were the drugs. It had been coming for months, and the home detox kit that Tori and I had bought got us off to a good start. We were both happy that our bodies felt clean and almost healthy, feelings which helped distract our minds from the thought that life without serious stimulation was beginning to look like a slightly less than exciting option neither of us were sure that we could stick to. But then, after that night in the church, phase two kicked in; I simply stopped wanting to get off my face. No more desire and no more drugs. I know it sounds like a convenient half-truth, and I still struggle with the fact right now, even after five months. Ian's been trying to quit the class As for a while and the poor lad's struggling. He's on a constant treadmill of feeling bad because he's hooked, then feeling bad because he's not high. He's had enough of feeling like a hamster in a cage but breaking free is just plain difficult for him. Me? Five minutes of mental madness and I'm clean. Sometimes life just isn't fair.

This whole Kiss 102 thing has helped too. I got the call when Zarc put my name forward to one of his mates who worked at the station. The regular gospel-led show had been dropped and the space had my name on. Sort of. I had to blag it that I could drive a desk, that I knew all about broadcasting and that my spiritual credentials were top notch. On every count it was just like being back in Alicante telling José Carlos that I'd grown up on the wheels of steel. He saw right through me and the same could be said for the boys at Kiss. Still, enthusiasm has always been the one thing that I haven't had to fake and I reckon it was that which won me through in the end.

I was reading a piece about Manumission the other day. The owners were saying how it all started in Manchester and was going well until the violence got too much. The final straw was when one of their crew got doused with petrol, set on fire and kicked down the stairs at the club. It was Salford that did it, trying to muscle in and take over the doors. Anyway, the point is that I remember being at the club that night. I didn't know the unlucky guy who was selected to be the Red Arrows demo for the Salford hard lads, but I can remember being in the queue to get in and seeing it all kick off. My point in mentioning it? I was there, but I don't remember *being* there. These recollections of mine almost seem like they've been borrowed, like they happened to another person. You see, so many of the experiences – in fact all of the drugged-up highs – were about living life in the present. With a couple of grams of charlie up your nose there is no tomorrow. Ecstasy is always just about the moment, the now, the tingles and rushes freezing time for a moment. A few years pass and these experiences become memories, but they remain isolated, separate from the rest of the action. I don't know, maybe I just took too much and realigned one too many neural pathways.

Things with Tori have been different too. We're still together, and I've got a feeling this one's for life, but the basic ingredients of Cam seem to her to have changed. I tell her I'm worried that she's finding all this change too much.

'Cam,' she said to me last night, 'I could cope with you high, I could cope with you stoned. I could even cope with you when you had your head in that book about world religions. I think I can cope with this.'

But is that it? Is that the Ascension? The eternal high suitably chopped and lined up, have I filled my hooter good and proper with more of the same? Have I just substituted one addiction for another? Have I just climbed up the same mountain I'd been up before but by a different route? I don't think so – but I would say that, wouldn't I? You know what this feels like? It feels nothing like a drug. There are no tingles, blips, buzzes or rushes. Compare it with the big boys and Christianity doesn't even register on the scale of sugar-sweet feelgoods. It's something else altogether, something deeper. Is it a high? If it is, it's the broadest one I've ever been on. I feel awake, content, happy with the way things are going. Life isn't just about preserving the moments of present-tense ecstasy, it's about purpose, meaning and everything else in between.

Back in the studio, Robert Owens telling Manchester just exactly why it is they can depend on him. I love that tune.

'This is Cameron Dante on Kiss 102 FM, with you for the next three hours bringing you the best uplifting house and garage.'

ASCENSION

On goes another tune; some white-label techno tune from Holland that I can't stand but told a mate's mate that I'd give it a spin on air as a favour. I'll give this one a miss so I stand back from the decks, pushing the headphones down onto my neck.

Could I tell my life story in the time it takes the record to play through?

'I was born. I got high. I went on the run. I came back. I went up. I went down. Up and down. Up and down. Joined the band. Got disillusioned. Met Tori. Gay scene. No cash. Stale clubs. Stale drugs. Stale career. Fresh start.'

Ten seconds! Not bad at all. But there's so much more to life than the bare facts. I don't even know if I could begin to describe what's in my head: so many possibilities, revelations, inspirations. What comes next in the plot? Who knows? Another go at the charts? Nah. Back out to play in clubs? Maybe. Whatever the case, it's got to be ME. No more hiding. No more games. No more being someone I'm not.

The first time I took acid, the time when Vinny and I bumped into the 'd'you wanna nut' crew, I sat on my bed getting freaked out about who exactly Cameron Dante was. When I finally went to sleep I dreamt that I was standing in a field next to some weird-looking bloke crouched over a slab of rock. He leant back and I could see it was a headstone. I knew that it was mine too. It wasn't frightening though, it wasn't like the bloke was trying to tell me when I was going to die. Instead he just pointed to the bit where the few lines describing me would go.

'What shall I write?' he asked.

Flashing light means there's an incoming phone call. That horrible scrunching sound means there's no time left on the turntable. No time to put a record on, so either I put it on live or broadcast pure silence while I change the record. I hope it's Ian on the line. Please God, let it be Ian and not some weirdo or a wrong number or something.

174

The Gap

'You're through to Cameron Dante on Kiss 102,' I say, trying not to sound too scared.

'Yeah' – it's not Ian, it's a woman – 'I've got a question for you.'

Please don't be insane. Please don't be insane. Please don't be insane.

'Oh right? What is it then?'

'Didn't you used to work out in Spain?'

'You know what, love, I've been thinking about that myself.'

USEFUL CONTACTS

Drugs help and advice
National Drugs Helpline
tel: 0800 776 600

Lifeline
101–103 Oldham Street
Manchester
M41LW
tel: 0161 839 2054
e-mail:
drughelp@lifeline.demon.co.uk

Housing aid
Shelter
88 Old Street
London
EC1V 9HU
tel: 020 7505 2000
e-mail:
manchester@shelter.org.uk

Rape and abuse help
1 in 4
219 Bromley Rd
London
SE6 2PG
tel: 020 8697 2112
website: www.oneinfour.org

Advice on related matters
Ascension
PO Box 159
Altrincham
WA14 2GU
tel: 0161 436 2714
e-mail: info@ascension-uk.com